"While there's life...there's still some fight left..."

I0148966

"Conflict"

Edited by Aaron & James Dalzell

Copyright © 2014 by Aaron James Dalzell

"The Man in the Arena" by Teddy Roosevelt

All Rights Reserved.

ISBN: 978-0692260487

Other Works Include:

Forgemaster (2013)

...by Candlelight (2014)

Trail of Flies (2014)

Off Road (2014)

CONFLICT

A Collection of Poetry

by

Aaron Dalzell

Contents:

I. In His Name

"The battle will not be over,

it will continue forever,

until blood has been spilled..."

5:06 a.m.

~

Nothing happens in the hours of 5:06 a.m.

nothing in the wee,

drawn out hours just before dawn,

that's when you start to hear the life reincarnate,

but it's the spring and summer I'm thinking of,

for there is no life,

out in the cold wasteland at wintertime,

January and February brood and drag,

graying the dawn in a mourning veil,

because breathing in the air this early,

makes me realize how stale I really am,

and how old I feel,

because no sleep,

just takes the life out of me,

no please don't,

don't issue me a *"Good Morning"*,

because I won't be up on time to hear it.

Dying Sandman

~

I can't go to sleep again,

those nightmares are crawling like spiders,

on paper-thin strands, line-drawn warnings in the sand,

I see the twisted faces, the skulls of dead enemies,

the gnarled bodies of human beings in pain,

suffering from their life that was insane,

I wished them dead, and now they come back,

they twist my reality, they mock me,

these ancient foes I see, they drive me closer to insanity,

I just want to close my eyes and sleep again,

I don't want to see those faces again...never again,

but I'm awake until my lullaby plays,

I'll be awake until the nightmares gut me,

until the nightmares have their revenge,

may the lullaby lead me on my way,

to lead me through the dark, for I am stranded,

I cannot find my way to inner peace, I cannot sleep,

the nightmares cut deep into the flesh and bleed,

they bleed the flesh of a dying sandman,

with no sandman, these insomniacs can never sleep...

Dawn the East

~

Daybreak,

first blush of morning light.

Time,

the beginning of a new delight.

East,

the reincarnation of a new divinity is reappearing.

Arising from the east, the first light is cast,

shifting through the skies, the camaraderie of the sun has past,

into the west, the illumine glides,

into the seas below the highest peaks,

from the gloom of the evening dusk,

shelter form the darkness of night,

the sun seeks...

Dusk,

last touch of evening light.

Time,

the decay of eternal life.

West,

into the depths of suffering.

Night,

into the earth the sun is sinking.

The Prologue

~

Second to last, one more to go,

there will be no more, after this one I'm through,

no more will I write to you from my house,

no more do I have anything to say to any of you,

I'll keep my voice my own, and speak alone.

For this kingdom I keep strong, this kingdom I rule,

I shall protect, I shall shelter,

I raise this shield so you cannot run me through,

no more to speak, nothing more can we do,

except, there is one more song,

one more thing that needs to be said,

that thing, is the mind inside my head,

that song, one more thought that needs to be read,

for your eyes alone, because mine have been fed,

ears have bled, fingers stricken with pain,

brain melting from the late night strains,

but this has got to stop, these messages are insane,

these pictures paint an idiots portrait,

one who doesn't know how to speak,

a face of you, a face of a fool,

trying hard, just doesn't cut it...I'm sick of trying,

like entertaining a group of locusts,

only they eat the paper I behold,

instead of reading the meaning it unfolds,

just need an epilogue to finish it,

to let you know that this time...I mean it!

A Simple Equation

~

It always starts out,

as a simple equation,

One plus one equals...?

This could be just numbers,

simple elementary math,

but I'm gonna say it's me and you,

too long has it been,

since I had a friend like you,

since the last time I saw you,

much has changed,

but one thing's for certain,

now that I rediscovered you,

I feel like it's going to add up,

and one plus one will equal out,

and the answer I get is two,

two is better than one,

maybe two is me and you,

but I should know better, and so should you!

Reflections

~

Reflections in life,

reflect our dreams,

what we desire, never comes to be,

what we dream, is up to us,

to make come true,

but dreams never turn out,

the way we want them to.

And our perception,

of what a reflection is,

differs to what we see,

in the reflection of a mirror,

for the background has been rearranged,

objects have been set in different places,

but I look the same, yet I do not see,

what I wanted to see,

this is not the way I wanted things to be,

nor is this what you wanted,

because what we truly want,

that which we desire,

is not me, is not you,

our dreams and fantasies are different,

we get what we don't want,

and loose what we want to keep close,

disappointed by what is waiting,

when we wake up,

you see me, when you wanted another,

you see me, when you wanted pleasure,

I see you, when I wanted love,

I see you, when I wanted a future for us...

Eyes in Line

~

Parallel eyes, look to the other,

eye to eye, look at one another,

take comfort, in the uncomfort,

that you two hate one another,

the feeling is mutual, synchronization,

when one eye follows the other,

when one person hates the other,

disregard what makes one feel,

what makes one think, about the other,

we can clearly see, these two hate each other,

when eyes spark in the dark with fire,

when the hate burns in one another,

when one eye, looks at the other...

Enigma

~

The enigma is a puzzle,

an interesting, thought provoking game,

when you're the question,

and no one has the answer,

what is it I think, what is it I feel?

Sometimes I don't know,

sometimes nothing seems real,

but I know I can love,

yet it's hard for me to relate,

we desire that special someone,

we want to be with that someone,

who makes our eyes light up,

in the darkest hours,

the beacon of light, to brighten up the day,

but first I need to be able to feel,

please stop, everyone is fifty steps ahead,

I need to know what that love feels like,

what care is taken as it caresses across the flesh,

it's an enigma, a puzzle, I do not understand,

a thought I cannot put to rest.

The enigma is a paradox,

a question that sometimes,

doesn't need to make any sense,

people and events just are, 99% of the time,

they don't make any sense,

love, life, death...sharing a moment,

hand in hand, in the pouring rain,

life just happens,

it's a puzzle sure, but like anything,

it's a puzzle that needs to be complete,

it's just a game I know not the rules,

I cannot contemplate,

the way life goes, and the way things turn out,

when two lives are fated to meet,

it will always be an enigma to me,

I think within me, there is a piece of that puzzle,

still missing...

Fornever

~

Does the subject still exist after forever?

Are the faces truly erased,

not from memory, but from familiarity?

Is the story of us gone,

with no happily ever after?

Stories tend to change and plots thicken,

take a turn for the worst, and sink in quicksand,

tales dumbed down by expectations,

some may think, they know what happens,

only the further onwards they go,

they'll soon come to realize,

they were disappointed.

The grass on the other side,

is the same barren desolation,

we stand upon today.

But I don't want to be disappointed,

I want to be sure, that where you stand today,

you'll be there tomorrow, and ever after,

that's not how it works though,

for we have our own road to follow,

our own role in the play.

Will I see you the next day, or tomorrow after?

Or will this story be the last chapter?

And when you leave,

is this going to be our undoing?

I wish we lived a fairy-tale,

I wish I was dreaming,

then I could alter our fate,

then we could have a happy ending.

At the Door

~

I'm still standing here,

standing here like I always have before,

you best move on with your life,

cause I'm patient,

and I'll just keep you waiting,

I'm in no hurry anymore,

I will not take that last step,

I will not rush out the door,

I am not welcome, don't invite me in,

I'm not taking chances anymore.

I'll just keep on standing here,

waiting at the door,

we can stride along side by side,

if you choose to, but your speed is faster,

and I'll be going at my own pace,

I have no stake in the outcome of this race,

to rush in, to be disgraced, to be brought down,

I won't take the risk anymore,

instead I'll just hang out over here,

on the other side of the door...

Talk Banter to Me

~

Talk banter to me,

say it nice and loud,

so that I can hear the pleasure,

tease me with your banter,

so that I can feel the pain later,

shout your banter nice and loud,

so that I can sleep at night, for I am restless,

and my body feels cold as ice,

if you melted me with your warmth,

it would feel so nice!

I can't read your banter,

it's subliminal to my ears, and my eyes, they lie,

the way you show yourself off,

You lie! You deny!

You defile my feelings with your lust,

so how can you feel anything with my touch?

When you want no love,

no emotion, for you refuse to trust!

Talk banter to me,

say something to reassure me,

say there will be pleasure,

you're all talk,

all you do is torture with your banter,

you tease me now and then reject me later,

but it doesn't matter now, because your gone,

and I no longer have to hear that useless banter!

You were nothing more than an agitator!

Fatality

~

Blood begins to boil,

and the anger and aggression is rising,

I don't know how to suppress these twisted visions,

they don't seem real,

I feel like I'm someone else, the real me has fallen asleep,

how can I explain this aggravation, it's like I don't exist,

just a mist that hovers over a pool of boiling water,

steam in the form of an apparition of myself,

can you see through me?

Can you read me,

can you hear every word and feel my hot breath,

as my mouth is churning, grunting and roaring!

I feel like the razorback, as the hunt closes in, surrounding me,

pushing me backwards, until I'm trapped in the corner,

I cannot escape,

I cannot run, cannot move, helpless from being subdued,

I cannot breath, I cannot shake this ugly feeling,

that when we see ourselves, eye to eye,

you hate me just the same,

but I hate you more, the closer you get to me,

but why do you smile, just to deceive me,

I cannot handle these words you spill,

like a laceration to my chest, an wrecking-ball to the face,

I spill my words back, like spitting blood and teeth,

that splatter all over the place,

for love and affection I cannot handle,

I don't like the way this fiend looks at me,

I just want to go back to the way things were,

before I received the final attack,

for love is not reality, affection is insanity,

sensuality...nothing more than dreamscapes,

and adolescent fantasies,

these emotions, that captivate me,

and make me feel warm inside,

are my deadliest fatality...

they tear me apart, as she turns me into a man,

I don't want to be...

True Love

~

These are my true love,

these treasures cement my destiny,

give me the drive and passion to be,

what I have always wanted to be,

these...these are all I need.

The pen and the paper does for me,

what no one else ever will,

bring joy, a smile, a tear, and a chuckle,

these lifeless objects,

do what other people never have,

living beings never gave me,

this spark in my life.

The pen and paper,

help me through troubled times,

they have always been there for me,

they listen to my thoughts,

as I write them down,

for they remember every moment,

every thought I write down,

they are not a metaphor,

for that special someone,

for there is no one there,

never any support for me,

these objects I accept as they are,

for no others have ever accepted me...

Pin Cushion

~

I may hold this intense look,

but some things never give,

a hard shell will never soften,

memories burned from anger,

will forever boil,

pain is always there,

some scars never heal,

unless help comes,

but...that help never will.

Life never gives,

it always takes,

and leaves a pin,

in its place.

I may hold these intense emotions,

I may be blinded by my rage,

but if there was just a sense of order,

someone, a helping hand,

to make me feel stronger,

but a hard shell never softens,

from the constant attacks,

and I spurn the friendly faces of today,

for the ones from yesterday,

have made my stomach turn,

something's...life and love,

they never give, it's a taking game,

how much pain, how much guilt,

how much shit day after day,

can I take?!

Love never gives,

it's a lie...a fake,

and when it leaves...it's gone,

only a pin to remind me of the pain...

remains in its place...

A Faded Memory

~

She's just a faded image,

a mistake I will erase,

she left, there was no explanation,

the only hard part,

I'm not asleep...I am awake,

maybe if I kept my eyes open,

I would have seen this coming,

for now I see her fading away,

she left without warning,

I guess the sun,

will hide behind the clouds this morning.

The Epilogue

~

It is done, the time has come at last,

the final hurrah, the words spoken here,

have come in last,

to shutter the tongue, and silence the voice,

when done with a day, a life,

that drags us down, we have one choice,

which way to go, which direction,

can we divide ourselves in,

where can death be reborn,

once we have killed the hours,

spent the time like gluttons and whores,

decide for yourself,

because I am safe where I belong,

I shall continue down this road alone,

let bygones be bygones, I am not concerned,

about the race lost in time,

the competition rules I defied,

let this past we kept alive corrode,

familiar faces, a wisp of dust in the road,

the wind will take the dirt away,

take it to the place where dreams go to die,

taken to where left-over bird feathers lie,

forgotten on the wayside,

while the sparrow flies free,

leaves his hope to laugh at me,

for I cannot fly, I have no wings,

let the chorus sing of the day that is to be,

when I forget about you, and you forget about me,

let the swansong dance to the music of the coda,

let this epilogue end a friendship,

where it should have,

when it could have, when it would have,

let the dirt and rust settle over a golden opportunity,

take what you can get out of life now,

because I reached my hand in blindly,

and I pulled out nothing,

give this lad a medal,

because he sure as hell tried,

look at him, filled with promise in his eagle eyes,

should of had the gold, but took a step back,

took the shortcut and cut some slack,

can he get a silver, nope...too damn bad,

he had his chance, he had his time, he threw it away,

to consume his life away from others,

they're a bother, no concern for others,

can he at least get a bronze, he gave it his best,

is the competition over with? Is there nothing else left?!

Smashed under rocks I could not lift,

drowned in water that was far too deep,

but it wasn't enough...it wasn't what I needed to do,

but what is the right interpretation of all of you,

give me a clue, on what the secret is?

Or is that the mystery,

is that the ancient secret buried in the sand?

Am I just supposed to go dig it up with my bare hands,

when everyone else has a shovel,

Hell, I built my shovel, turned it into a bulldozer,

dug for hours and hours, only to find an empty pit,

and inside was a note that read loneliness,

you lose, sorry you missed the exit,

you have to keep running, for all eternity,

only fools go looking, I guess I'm the jester,

the mime, the clown,

I guess I can't help but keep getting knocked down,

and slammed into the dirt,

that's why I wear black,

to cover up all that filth, and hide the blood,

blood from scars of a personal flood,

consisted of tears and empty hands,

worked for promises that never came to be,

I guess that's why I love the make believe,

I guess that's why I love to see my reflection in a dream,

because if there is anywhere I can go,

to escape life and be with the people that truly care,

the people in my mind, that I make up, that I define,

selfish it may be, but that's how my life goes,

when I turn around crying,

I can always imagine that perfect home,

that perfect place where everyone is there,

and they welcome me,

they welcome me home,

in my mind I'm not alone,

I am sufficient, locked away in sleep,

nothing can touch me, nothing can hurt me,

until I hear the call, the alarms sound,

they wake me up, into this nightmare,

they drag me back into this disgusting reality,

of yesterdays and miserable years to ponder,

and wonder where it all went wrong, why am I behind?

Why must I continue trying, why can't I succeed?

When will life quit punishing me?!

It's bitter sweet,

for sleep brings on tomorrow,

and that may be why I never can rest,

and at the end of this epilogue,

is the conclusion, the closure,

on a profile of bitterness & sorrow

about a child who should be a man,

a man who has no hope for tomorrow...

Flaminian Gate

~

On his feast day, we celebrate,

with candy hearts and,

manufactured "Love You" cards,

false materials,

produced solely for corporate gain,

is this how we treat a martyr?

Is this how we commemorate,

one who after beaten by clubs,

and pummeled with stones,

refused to give up his faith?

Is a box of chocolate hearts,

and lingerie, and gift cards,

really the only possessions,

we think of on St. Valentine's day?

A man who showed,

that love is not just physical possession,

but it's the power of the word,

the strength of devotion,

it's not once a year we should say we love,

it's not once a year,

we should stick to what we feel is right,

it's a lifetime of struggle and fighting,

devoted to what we believe,

what makes us who we are inside,

forget the two or three words,

drawn on wrappers,

and etched on candy,

these are feelings that should just be innate,

they should never pass,

we can't forget what love actually means,

devotion always to who and what we truly need,

the love to be felt,

in whatever way is best for you and me.

The vows and a wedding ring,

can't hold a candle,

to the beheading of a saint by the guillotine,

for doing what he knew was right in his heart,

a real heart that bled, not a red paper shape,

not a cartoon heart,

to symbolize a holiday we've maimed!

This man was St. Valentine,

you all know the holiday,

but do you know his name,

he knew the meaning of true love,

he proved his devotion,

by being executed,

in front of the Flaminian Gates.

So throw your flowers,

and Hallmark cards away,

and say to those who mean the most to you,

"I love you and I'd die for you!"

Not once a year on February 14th,

but every...single...day!

The Kiss of Forever

~

One kiss goodnight,

is all I ask,

just one kiss,

feel your lips upon my neck,

love me temptress,

lure me with those eyes,

just one kiss, and my hands are tied,

look at us, eyes upon one another,

love me temptress, love me forever...

Eternal Love
(Love Never Dies pt. II)

~

There is blood on the horizon,

I smell the sweet iron nectar on the wind,

that's when the nightmares come out,

in our sleep, they watch us,

in our minds, they stalk us,

of our sanity, they relieve us,

but there is something,

a sweeter, more perfume scent,

a luring essence I cannot deny,

for the warning in my heart has died,

for I am in comfort of this female I spy,

and that's when I meet her,

the most beautiful creature,

I have ever laid eyes upon,

a succubus with the scarlet, forked tongue,

she comes to me, sailing across sunless skies,

to carry me away, upon daemonic wings,

and I bask into her eyes, and by her love I am petrified,

for we stand together side by side,

overlooking a land of ash and the rising blood-tide.

I her king, and she my bride,

our wedding held on the blackest day,

without clandestine,

a celebration of the unholiest kind,

we consummate, our cold bodies intertwined,

like two snakes entangled among the vines,

charring the hawthorns we despise,

burning the plant that tries to subdue,

attempting to stop a love that is true,

for I would die for her, I would take the blade for her,

and let the steel run me through,

let the stake destroy me,

I taste the blood as it drizzles,

from the nape of her neck,

and she ravishes me,

a beating heart of bliss and ecstasy,

and a child shall be born, into a faded existence,

but the love for this child, will be no different,

she is ours, a daughter bound by blood for magnificence,

and she will crush all resistance,

just as her mother, just as I...

for she is hers, and she is mine.

Somber is the mood, of pale light under a full moon,

and we stand together hand in hand,

and we will rule together,

as our darkness wraps around,

tightens its grip upon the land,

we were made for each other she and I,

the perfect pair, we are immortal,

our love is eternal, our love shall never die!

This I vow, under the watchful eyes above,

for no army, no siege, no empires, no sorcery,

you cannot come between unconditional love,

for she loves me, and it is my queen of the night I love...

Too Many Doors Closed

~

Give me a chance,

just some space and time,

always put me on the line,

make the pressure boil over,

the spout cries and yells,

weeps of its death, and then expels,

steam is hot when panic stricken,

the seas roar, and tidal waves sore,

the water bubbles and tips the scale too far,

and I hoist my sail, when the winds not right,

the compass needle goes haywire,

I wreck upon the distant shore,

I thought the backdrop was an eternal bliss,

a new adventure into the mist,

order bows to rage,

skin glows volcanic underneath,

when I'm engaged with more,

no more I ask, no more can I take,

just let the water settle, just let the pressure break,

open up the gates, release the flow,

is there a peaceful sea I can just..drift upon,

I'd like to know,

is there a door, that isn't closed?

Is there a right direction,

without a wrong way to go?

I look outside, through the key hole,

just to see that small hope,

that there will be no more sorrow,

and the new world on the horizon,

will bring with the tides,

a better tomorrow...

This is Not an Entrance

~

There is no entrance when you always run,

there is no finish,

when you quit what is not done,

I run so much, I've lost so many opportunities,

I've quit so much,

I feel as though I never started.

Seems like the exits are always open,

always going, nothing ever showing.

Success comes in slow increments,

that I realize now,

I just wish I could keep going,

I just want to make it,

I just wish I knew how.

"...and Life asked..."

~

...and Life asked Death,

"Why do people love me, yet hate you?"

Death responded,

"Because you are a beautiful lie...

and I am a painful truth."

Chronicalogic

~

I was born, when I accepted my fate,
day after day, hazed and banished,
crawling on my hands and knees,
through a never ending maze,
the feeling of being slapped,
a swipe across my face,
I wish the heat from the pain,
was the heat one feels,
from another's embrace.

I will die, I accepted my fate,
fighting through the crowds,
and bullshit day after day,
punish me some more?
I'll receive more than I can take,
and I'll feel the blows some more,
I'll take the full force of hate.
Am I a mirror?

Can you see the reflection,

of yourself in my eyes?

Paint the bull's-eye on me,

and I'll be your target to beat!

The weak are eaten alive,

the respectful are the ones who hurt,

we have the eyes that cry,

we'll be the ones to die,

because it's only logical,

that the rude and hurtful live on,

immortality was never meant for me,

have you ever seen a god that's weak?

Didn't think so.

The gods eat the mortals,

the gods abuse the fearful.

Are you a mortal, are you fearful?

Having doubts...is what gives us bravery,

having tears...it what lets us feel,

having fear...is what gives us strength,

being confused...will help us think,

thoughts are the only logic a brain needs,

do you think, do you feel,

when you're stabbed in the back,

is it blood you spill?

Do you bleed,

when they peel away the scab that heals,

do you protect...do you run and flee?

It's ok if you do,

for I do and I'm not afraid to say so,

because all these emotions that I feel,

these feelings, mean I'm alive,

I may scream and yell...

but I never harm or defile,

I may fail, sometimes I succeed...logically,

this is the way it should be,

I'm a creature of chance,

I never know what's next,

living day by day,

curious of the future that lays ahead,

not afraid to cry,

not afraid to bend and learn something new,

and I'm not afraid to admit,

I have never felt true love,

because I was never given the chance,

to take the chronological steps,

and present myself to someone,

not as a fake, or a plastic doll,

with a smile on my face drawn by paint.

But to be myself, to be real,

I am real...my flesh is alive,

biologically... it will rot when I die.

I was born, I was not early nor was I late,

it was just right...for the person I am,

to go through life,

and learn the lessons and make the mistakes,

to be a smarter man toady,

than the child I was yesterday.

I learned a few things that you may not know,

if I am slapped, I do not hit back,

for I am passive, and that's a biological fact,

we cannot change who we are and how we act,

if you want a fight, I won't fight back,

if you call me a name, I'll smile and turn,

I won't look back,

I'll just think you're a no-good ass!

I have a heart, most women don't understand,

that it's the ugly ones that use their back-hand,

I have respect, and the toughness I lack,

if that pushes the girl of my dreams away,

it's ok because,

I don't need her dragging me down,

and holding me back.

Life has been the greatest teacher,

for my teachers were scum,

they could find the weakness of a helpless child,

and exploit it, let the crack break,

and the rapids of a lifetime,

of pain break through,

some bruises heal, some never do,

some wounds I'm still licking,

wounds that I out-grew,

yet the tainted memories are still there,

the taste of blood still lingers,

from biting my tongue,

the past still isn't through...it's never over.

I was born...and I will die,

it's too early to decide my fate,

but it's too late for correcting any old mistakes,

it's ok, because all I've learned,

is from mistakes,

the next time I'll know...

I don't want to stay the same,

our evolution, our growth, is not without pain,

and chronologically...

that's the way it's supposed to be,

after all...we are human beings,

birth_life_death...

this is the timeline of mortality,

for not even the writing on our tombstone,

is immortal, for by the lips of nature,

the wind will blow,

and the name we were born with yesterday,

will fade away tomorrow...

Re_Con_Nec_Ted

~

I feel as though I've been re-directed,

taken down another road,

while my brain tends to stray,

I've taken another path,

started learning another lesson,

hoping that I'll find another piece,

and become re-con_nec-ted.

Maybe I'll stick to this way,

maybe I'll learn something new,

I wish I had an extra life in the game,

I've been given one too few,

I guess I'll just have to make due,

and stick with what I'm able to do,

maybe this is the right direction,

another piece found,

and I'm becoming recon_nec-ted.

I finally see, the sun shine above the horizon,

but I need to keep the sunglasses on,

I can't see into the future,

it's hard enough,

to see what's in front of me today,

my blurred vision is becoming clear,

and the decay I once felt, is nothing more,

than a broken reflection in a dirty mirror,

I'm a singular person, living on a single life,

but this game is not yet over,

there's still more to discover,

by the past, I have been rejected,

yet this pushes me to look at tomorrow,

and become recon_nected.

Too long, I've felt so disconnected,

feeling pulled apart, cut into a million pieces,

been made promises,

and came out of the game empty-handed,

with nothing but my own pride,

to show for what is accomplished,

my mind feels,

it needs to go in another direction,

let go of the past, and release the rage at last,

a hand to hold,

and I'll no longer be disconnected,

I think I've done something,

to become one with myself, and be acceptant,

of who I am...and become reconnected.

No More Encores

~

I want to continue,

but it's useless to sing a song to deaf ears,

there's no need to play the tune,

to share with those who never listen,

is there a point, to continue with the encore,

to the empty seats at the show?

I just have one final act,

one scene left in the play,

I'll recite my lines one more time,

and then it's time for me to go.

Source of the River

~

Let's go back, to when this began,

life's beginnings, when time was simple,

children with buckets and shovels,

building castles in the sand,

worlds created with imagination,

empires ruled by ancient civilizations,

swimming across oceans with no limitations,

the land on the horizon,

a golden-green salvation,

life was simple without complications,

the truth concealed, to stop the bleeding easier,

the hurt withdrawn,

so the tears would dry faster,

but now we're older,

and the river is moving on,

we're swimming faster,

crossing this ocean is becoming harder,

the stream's a bit wider,

the tides are coming in stronger,

and we're dragged out further,

getting our feet wet, then up to the shins,

the water is getting deeper,

the waves are getting higher,

but we paddle harder, we're getting stronger,

for everything has a beginning,

a middle, and an ending,

if life was easy, we'd be weak, we'd be helpless,

when we truly needed the strength,

we would never be ready,

we would falter,

we'd dig our hole deeper and deeper,

the strength we carry today,

comes from its source,

we can trace it back to the beginning,

when life was simple,

children floating on an inner tube,

drifting on further,

lower the sails, and drift with the current,

hold the moment,

this life doesn't need to go any faster,

enjoy the days,

when the summer vacation lasts forever,

back when life was simple,

back at the beginning,

our lives have to start somewhere,

when we're at the docks,

looking out across that vast and endless sea,

kick off hard, life is the journey forward,

there's a long voyage ahead,

endless it may seem,

but the summer days will start to feel shorter,

so just glide along on the endless stream,

enjoy the ride, and smile,

at the beginnings of a dream,

never forget what you see yourself to be,

dreams can soar,

they can just as quickly crumble at the seams,

so let's go back to the beginning,

when life was simple and filled with dreams,

dreams were all we needed,

dreams were in reality, what destiny is to be,

life is never what it seems,

as chaotic as the ripples in this stream,

life is never what it seems,

we cannot control life,

the way we can control our dreams,

but it is up to us, to turn our dreams into reality,

we can only float, for this river will never cease,

but no matter where the river goes,

it all starts with a source,

and where the river ends up,

well, we'll just have to sail onward,

and see what we're in for,

read the ancient writings,

of those civilizations that came before,

learn a thing or two along the way,

and where we'll go,

it all comes full circle,

it all dates back to the source…

Liquid Earth, On Solid Seas

~

The world, it appears backwards to me,

like liquid earth, thrust against solid seas,

for the daytime is slumber,

and by night I linger,

only to see another moment falter,

it's life, and that's how it goes,

there is opportunity, that much I know,

but unless I search, it never shows,

this lingering is my existence I suppose,

never reaching out to opportunity when it shows,

watch as the ships sail by,

just stand at the dock and watch life pass me by...

Roadwork Ahead

~

I can read the sign, see the red flags waving,

they warn me of what's up ahead,

rocky roads, and broken asphalt,

there is no smooth passage I'm afraid,

no steam rollers or road crew can fix this mess,

I got myself caught in this traffic jam again,

the orange cones don't guide me,

because I'm stuck in the left lane,

they confine me to one path,

I need to make that right,

I need to make things right,

I need to smooth things over,

I have no direction, nowhere do I want to go,

no destination,

and I know that on this road, the further I go,

there's gonna be more work needed,

more cause to watch the signs and pay attention,

this broken highway is in need of repair,

I need to fix these bumps and potholes,

repaint the yellow lines,

that have almost disappeared,

so there's no more detours,

just one direction best for me,

to focus on my journey ahead,

but this is a one-lane road, one way,

for there's no coming back again.

You see, that's why these roads have detours,

because there's no going in reverse,

if I forgot something before I left,

I can't go back and get it,

I just have to make due,

and drive on through the green lights,

and be sure to yield when necessary,

stop just a little short at the red lights,

for there may be some danger,

red was always the warning,

and sometimes we gotta slow down,

and make those little stops to regain ourselves,

because this route is a long one,

hope I picked up all I need.

If not, I'll just have to wait and see,

what there is waiting for me,

what will I discover,

what will I find when I reach that destination?

There's a long road ahead of me...

Bum-Bee

~

I feel the scars, you try to hide,

but I can see the pain,

the bitterness on the inside,

for I know it too, I know it all too well,

you do your best, the best you know how,

support the weight of the world,

upon your iron shoulders,

"...we'll do better, we'll get ourselves together

It'll take time, to get ourselves organized...

you're doing fine, it'll get better..."

hold the strength of me together,

we share our blood, we shed the same tears,

cry tears with me, we'll cry a river,

I empathize, I sympathize,

I am you, who else could I be

I know you'll be there forever,

I know your there for me...

"I love you son...forever..."

Only a Thought
(The Sun)
~

Can I make the seasons change

will this snow around me, confining me,

ever melt away, bring on that spring I need in my day,

will those gray clouds part,

and no longer, will my mind linger in the haze.

Will the sun come back again,

come out and wave its tender arms to me,

say it's alright, the day's still bright,

can the summer come sooner, just last a little longer,

because the days don't feel warm anymore.

Are things ever going to change,

I take the steps and make the mistakes,

am I learning more, or changing for the worse,

could life be just a little bit different, I don't ask for much,

feel the winds of autumn on a clear spring day.

Will this mist dissipate after the rain,

I guess this means the days are getting warmer,

but I'm still cold, I still feel that chill,

weep across the chip in my shoulder,

I just want to see what it is I'm missing.

I think the mist is clearing,

I can open my eyes a little bit wider,

because I can sleep just a little bit better,

I just want to stay awake and enjoy the day,

walk in the sunshine,

enjoy this time I have, and live this life,

the only change I ask, is to be a little stronger.

Heart of Gold

~

Strong and tough,

able to bend every which way,

a smile as bright as its shining glow,

to bring joy to each and every day!

A symbol of good and a role model for life,

pumping the blood of serenity,

through each vein,

a river of gold, relieved of strife.

Good times, are never bad,

its bond fire burns,

forever with a loving warmth,

of happiness and being glad,

to be alive each day!

The strength of the mightiest wall,

of steel and stone,

and a gate of the strongest oak,

to forever stand tall.

Its limbs reach out all around the world,

to lend a hand,

to recuperate and revitalize one and all,

to a stature of being proud.

Depression is in no way a strong belief,

starting over and fresh, to not give up,

is salvation over the enemy, grief.

Forever and ever, to whatever nightmares,

and dreams may come, a heart of gold,

will rise up, and save this majestic kingdom.

A heart of gold will always pull through!

Frame 12welve

~

The ball is rolled at a swift speed,

tearing the pins apart,

sweeping them off their feet.

The pins explode with the sound of thunder,

one soaring through the air into the gutter.

There the pins lay, for eleven in a row,

The people gather all around,

and watch my clean sweep, to twelve I go!

The pressure is on my shoulders,

my breathing is heavy, the lights are bright.

I stare down the lane in a gaze,

take a deep breath, empty my mind,

and catch the pins in my sight.

The ball rolls at a swift speed,

tearing the pins apart,

sweeping all but one...off their feet!

Humanchines

~

0000011110010101010001001010101010100100

0101We are all parts, robotics, and physics,1

gears turning, wheels spinning,100001111001

an apparatus 24/700010001100001010011110

at the core, the processor is constantly,10101

producing new information,01000110000010

new tasks to be completed,1000100001001111

more work to be done,101000000111111110000

in a timely manner, with perfect symmetry,001

on time and parallel to what is going on,11111

there is no excuse when not going too far,0101

sensory overload, then we shutdown,11100011

yet the world keeps moving on,0011110000110

even machines need a rest some-days000111100

10101001011000100010001010101010011111001

01110000000000000011111111000001111001101

1111001001000111........................... : - (

DYE

~

What color shall I be today?

A pale white,

or a pleasant shade of gray?

Shall I keep a heart as black as coal,

or shall I bleed red, a soft maroon?

Does my heart glisten,

like a summer afternoon?

Will the dark circles,

of my eyes consume,

and eclipse the full moon?

What is there to see today,

when the color I am,

shows what I want to say.

Maybe I'll lay back,

and burn in the sun,

when flesh sizzles and crisps,

and the ashes gray,

blow away from the wind of a kiss...

The Opera

~

Set the stage, hit the lights,

for there is a power in the air tonight,

there is an aura shining bright,

it's like a power, the forces of the universe,

a force that will never die, far surpass the end of time,

there is only one stage, let the show begin,

and we walk, the cast and crew, hand in hand,

when the show begins, we turn into actors,

we pretend not to know one another,

we play the parts, we take the audience in,

by the hand, feed them our lines,

we take in the sighs, the laughs, the tragedy,

the cries, the jokes, the animosity,

and when the act is through,

the climax falls,

we take the stage one last time,

we had our ups, we had our downs,

that's how the play was written,

that's how our parts were played,

we take our bow, receive the rounds of applause,

and then we turn from one another, we walk away,

but we did have our hugs, we said our good-byes,

blew a kiss to all, and wished all a goodnight,

for when the curtain falls,

upon an empty, back-lit stage,

and all the others have faded away,

I'm still standing there,

I have one last page,

I haven't finished,

the show is far from done,

the cast has left,

the audience is gone,

but I still have one more performance to put on,

so if you please, may I have your attention,

would you please listen,

hear these final words I have to say,

"Hear me loud, hear me clear,

for my volume was mute, and my voice,

less than a whisper, against these loud-mouth liars,

I have not been allowed to speak,

to say what I need to say,

and if you should care enough to listen,

then I will live out my life, act my part,

and continue to live day by day,

not in a play, not in my own fantasy,

but be myself, on the stage of reality,

in a world where there is no morality,

I will be the best performer, I will make it real,

I will belt out my lines, and show the emotions,

a genuine human should feel,

cry the tears of sadness, smile with happiness,

laugh with enjoyment, mourn with bereavement."

I will mourn the passing of time that has wasted,

but I'll let the weeping cease, I will continue this struggle,

of maintaining my credentials,

and finding the audience that will understand,

an audience I can keep, understanding of what they hear,

and what they see,

I will focus all energy, on a story that needs to be finished,

standing at attention, waiting for my opportune audition,

given the chance, reading the right lines,

and when the time is right, the curtains will open,

and it will be my time to shine...

Origami

~

Bent out of shape,

but who's counting the folds,

twisted and bent, to fill the mold,

out of shape, or so I am told,

identified by my actions,

to try and fit the mold,

image is unclear,

but change is reforming,

rearranging the different substances about me,

who and what I am is unclear,

but what I'm made of,

can be judged by the fourth sense,

change the structure,

rearrange the outside,

and the insides must alter,

there has to be a change,

contortion collides with friction,

of yet another fold,

another shape taken,

the structure starts to take hold,

the exterior is taking form,

a distinct shape becoming clear,

learn to appreciate that which is inside me,

and strengthen what I'm good at,

changing, by learning from fear,

an image is taking hold,

making sense out of all these folds,

plains rise into dunes, hills become mountains,

sky becomes space, infinite and timeless,

take a step upwards,

and embrace the imagination,

take the step back, and the folds undone,

and I'm back to the flat sheet of paper,

static without care for my behavior,

become the swan, grace when wings unfold,

become the eagle, pride soars high,

become the hawk, and watch from the sky,

I am not the shape, the shape is me,

I cannot be formed, the form I make,

I know what I am, I am not a shape,

I take on the form, of the life I make…

REV

~

Rev…rev it loud…LOUDER!

Rev…rev it high…HIGHER!

Put the pedal to the metal!

Hit the gas and go…GO FASTER…FASTER!

Don't stop till I lose control!

And paint the highway,

with a fresh coat of blood and oil!

Hear the roar of slicing generators,

register the mach's up to speed,

pistons thrust, diesel and gasoline,

boils within the bladder,

the smell of fuel lingers,

on my hands as they grip the wheel tighter,

rev the engines, to a faster high,

in10sity that breaks the vessels in my eyes,

and take the steel for a drive;

denounce the limits,

for nothing stands in my way,

between me and this asphalt, the playground,

a young man's never-ever land.

It's only the thrill I live for,

the faster the speed, the faster the heart beat,

"You only live once!" they say,

but I've decided I wanna die today,

slam down that pedal,

take this chance, and risk it all…

for I am the speed-demon!

The smell of burning tires,

and scorched road pleases the senses,

crank the stereo,

for I have the power over this machine,

at the wheel I'm in total control,

and no one's in control of me,

a speed junkie who just needs a hit,

the freedom to die at every turn,

keeps my youth alive,

I don't give a shit,

because I'm never gonna slow down,

I'm never gonna quit,

if I blink I crash, beware, I fear nothing,

for I have nothing to lose.

I'd rather die in this minute,

than live the rest of my days in a cage,

the engine purrs, the gaskets rattle,

I don't know how much more,

acceleration she can take,

I won't slow down! I refuse to hit the brakes!

I'm not worried; I don't regret my mistakes,

I kick-start the rpm's,

elevate the needle higher,

into the red it goes,

80...90...100...110...how much faster can I go,

this ain't enough, I need more power!

That's what it takes to quench my thirst,

here comes the sudden bend in the road,

I take this corner way too fast,

the shocks rattle, the brakes engulf in flames,

the pads are stripped and torn away,

metal clashes upon metal,

off road...through the guardrail, gasoline leaks,

a spark ignites us, in a ball of fire we explode,

the next stop is hell, and away we go!

Ground\/\/\Breaking

~

I want these words to be ground breaking!

Nothing new or fresh, not uplifting or amazing,

but to summon all catastrophe,

earthquakes and disaster,

to rip open the earth,

and tear away the crust and mantel,

tear down the buildings,

send the bones of civilization to the core,

swallow all life,

engulf all the oceans and the sky above,

drag all that matter down beneath,

burned by the riptide of lava,

that cleanses with flames,

burning the forests and cleansing the land,

washing the dying species away,

the skeleton of society has collapsed,

and the bones are smashed,

by the jaws of tectonic plates,

and the shifting of the land,

let the soil suffocate,

the gases choke, and the magma boil,

bury these fossils under the remaining dust,

and then the winds take the ashes,

and clear this day away,

and what is left after the earth's break-down,

surely it won't be us!

Never Let It Die

~

Never let it die,

just keep the river flowing...

for that's what keeps you going,

if there is a kindle becoming a flame,

give it some air, feed it bramble,

make the fire roar,

embrace the metamorphosis that takes place,

for this roaring fire, is an ember no more.

Never let the ideas go, never let the stories fade,

for like the child...within us, they are made,

never let the story die,

let your imagination keep soaring,

keep the waters pure,

and let this river keep on flowing.

Never let anyone say any different,

because you know where you're going,

never let the writing die,

for when you stand on top of the world,

you'll know just why,

it's because you never gave up,

you never let the effort within you die!

Altars of Time

~

Running down,

the sand is running out,

to the other side, circling clockwise,

downwards into a spiral,

a circle of infinity,

the hour glass circles,

in the reflection of mirrors,

altered by the ripples,

of the oceans in the eye,

yawning chasms in space and time,

catch the pieces left behind,

swallow away the ancient days,

swallow away the layout,

the fingerprints, of a bye gone age,

the sacrifice of culture, of values,

of instincts we so long understood,

evolving over centuries and eons,

changing with the tides,

while eternity is the measure,

of how many minutes,

are on the inside.

Is it Infinity?

~

Will this always last,

go on and on,

have we seen the last rays,

of the final dawn?

Will we speak of these days,

if we still see tomorrow,

yesterday has almost left us,

we're running out of time to borrow...

Distilled

~

It's always raining, the drops are ever pouring,

noticed like tear drops in a storm,

every flowing, never healing,

taste their saltiness, taste the pain that's sown,

into lives that never grow, fates we never sow,

weaves of lives transcend into artwork,

and the droplets of tears become drops of blood,

lives become death...and with every tear,

life will never grow, tears were never pure,

tears are sour, tears are bitter,

when we distill their essence, what is a tear?

Sadness from loss, and fear from being afraid,

sadness of misunderstanding,

the fear of abandonment,

I look out the window,

it's still raining...still pouring,

I close my eyes and sleep once more,

I still have tears that need to shed,

from all the memories I keep inside my head,

it's raining, it's pouring,

time for sleep...time for bed...

?

~

Can I confess something to you?

Can I explain my thoughts and feelings?

Or will you just stare at me,

will you be afraid,

once you know the dark side of me?

Can you handle what you may not know,

what you did not guess?

Can I appeal to your empathy,

and get my secrets off my chest?

Because I realize,

that you may not understand,

you will not be able,

to comprehend my feelings,

the way I do;

do you?

Will you?

1,000 Pages or 1,000 Words

~

"1 Word Over a 1,000 Times

Unspoken...Will Never be Heard."

If I wrote one word,

hidden within one thousand pages,

would you care enough to find it,

would you read it?

And if you did, would you believe it,

could I believe you?

Would you believe that one thought,

the one word I would say,

is what I think of you,

would you care enough to take the time,

and try to find what's been eating at my mind,

biting the cuts upon my tongue,

a silence falls like the shadows of a sinking sun,

would there be love, dismay, animosity,

discomfort, for the emotions I have for you,

romance, proven to be true,

proven to be you, proven to make me a fool,

could you help this lonely soul,

whose fate stands upon the balance of one word?

Or could I tip the scale, one by one,

and turn this world around,

turn your world upside-down,

type it word for word,

type one thousand words, and when it's all done,

would you care to pierce my shell and taste my soul,

taste the words I write upon your tongue,

read my emotions poured into the eldest scroll,

look deep into my heart and tell by description,

adjectives, and nouns, the verbs I spill,

could that tempt you, could I describe you,

about the way you look, the way I see you,

the way I know you, the way I know,

I want to love you, how you move,

how you walk, how you talk,

I dare not cause you pain, I do not stalk,

for I wish you no pain, no misery,

I enjoy when your smile, that light upon you face,

brightens my darkness, cast light into my shadows,

could I articulate my feelings with sound,

I dare not utter, for the stutter of fear is profound and ugly,

so I'll just write this all down, I'll jot the letters into sentence,

sentence into paragraphs, paragraphs into a fascination,

a work of confession, a crime of passion, a devoted obsession,

I don't want to do wrong, I want what is right,

but I don't know if the power is there,

for there is no response, a certain lack of temptation,

I see you as a work of art, not a creature I wish to scar,

I dare not change what is already perfect,

would I chip the marble from a whispered secret,

and if you said yes...would I believe it?

One thousand pages, one thousand words,

for there's one secret I keep hidden,

and I'm afraid to share it,

for I say to myself daily,

she'll only smile by laughing at it,

and so I shall abandon the dreams, the could-be's,

I'll let her move on, while I linger here,

and curse the day I ever said maybe...nah,

it can't be...not me...why would she ever like me?

I'll just ignore her, while she stands there waiting,

looking at me...it can't be, why would it be me she sees?

There's nothing special, nothing hidden inside me,

except for that one word, that one emotion I'm cursed with,

it's called caring...don't ever care like me,

it never gets you anywhere...look at the confidence it gives me?

And I know exactly what you're thinking...

"Pathetic...isn't he?"

I know...that's what she thinks, when she looks at me.

Eaten on the Inside

~

In the blood,

I feel it crawling inside me,

biting, burrowing through flesh,

eating away at me,

soon there will be nothing of me,

and I'll be left here sitting,

lifeless, as this parasite I've created,

has taken that which is most important away,

a life to lead, for none I have,

for this inner beast inside me,

has taken, eaten away the heart and mind,

leaving only a shell starring at white noise,

an empty, lifeless hermit,

living like a ghost in the daylight,

for all eternity!

Somewhere

~

I want to go somewhere,

somewhere far away,

somewhere no one can see me cry,

somewhere to go when I try to run away,

I want to go somewhere,

no one else can go,

until I realize when I turn around,

and no one is there,

that's when I realize I am alone,

no one wants to be near me,

no one loves me enough to follow,

I'm in a place that no one else can see,

I'm invisible to the eyes of morality,

I'm a figment of imagination,

a human unlike any other,

in my place somewhere, I discover,

I can never return to the status quo...

I can never recover the balance....

I can never again, be around another....

I can never be around them,

I can never be around you,

when I leave to the place I go,

all that will be left of me,

are my tracks left in the ashes,

gray as summer rain, and cold as snow,

don't bother to follow,

because the door is closed,

the gates are locked, and within my eyes,

you will see, that no one is home,

no one will answer, because I left,

I went to that place, somewhere far away,

and in that corner of my mind,

I will forever remain, and I will cry in sorrow,

that is my fate, these are the final days,

what was left of the man you see is gone,

because when what's done is done,

nothing else remains...

Gray Days under Blue Sky

~

Feeling the worst,

under clear blue sky,

with just a hint of gray,

on traces of clouds pass by,

the smile of the sun,

reflects a glint,

of the tears in my eyes,

the grass it dances,

by the music of the winds,

happy to be in bloom this season,

while I linger on,

wandering under my clouded dome,

thoughts to myself,

just me and the band playing on the stereo,

unsung and all alone,

the song I hear,

the notes they play,

is a dull, depressing tune,

reflecting my thoughts,

reflecting in my mind,

the voice is mocking,

the words they don't lie,

and I can't deny,

they know how it feels,

they know the signs,

their words speak true,

of how it feels to be trapped inside,

it's not even midday,

it's only youth,

the day is young at noon,

the day's not over with,

but already I'm done,

I don't share the pleasure,

in the smile of the sun,

feeling gray, under a clear blue sky,

nothing more than a stone,

a lifeless statue,

dull and faded against the light,

Spring is in gloom,

it's only twelve noon,

life can't be done this soon,

it's only twelve noon,

what's wrong with life,

what am I to do,

life can't be over with,

it's only twelve noon,

it's too soon...too soon,

the funeral home is in view,

the sign like a movie poster,

it's mocking me...calling me,

the tabloids read:

"...Coming Soon, in this Life of Doom!"

and my name is up there,

under lights and a clear blue sky,

judgment of the future,

is written in the eyes of the past,

what else is there to say,

when blue skies start to gray...

The Only Road Home

~

The only place I know,

is a place far from the unknown,

located down a stretch of lonely road,

it won't be long now, soon I'll be home.

Some ideas of where we go,

is a place we live, a place we call our own,

but I have no house,

I have nowhere to call my own,

I only live to exist, to travel this solitary road.

There's only one way to go,

I can't be sidetracked, I know what is in store,

for me and what's my own,

who I am a man who walks alone,

I packed my bags, I carry my load,

I'll keep on going, till I sleep under my stone.

There is a place I know,

a place that's close, because I know,

how to find my way,

down this stretch of lonely road,

a ghost of who I once was, a shadow who walks,

in a mind that's all my own.

Home is an idea, and my idea of where I belong,

is a place to myself, for I am the solitary ghost,

that no one sees as he makes his way,

down this somber road,

no regrets, I choose the way I go,

my decision is all my own.

With none standing beside me,

I'll always walk alone.

Home is where the heart is,

my heart has been left out in the cold,

soon I will lay next to my name,

carved upon the stone.

There is only one life,

there is only one road home,

this is my path, my long walk alone,

it won't be long now,

just a few more miles to go…

Mental Instincts

~

It's always so easy isn't it?

to know exactly who you are,

what you want to be,

to be so perfect,

as though you were assembled by the gods,

your limbs sewn together by golden threads,

and a perfect, all-knowing,

brain encased within your head.

But do you really know who you are?

Do you have…any idea of life's true destiny?

Or what's in store for you and me?

Do you follow your mental instincts,

to be who you were born to be?

Or do you follow your faith blindly?

Breaking Conventions

~

I walk in no one's footsteps,

I have my own glory,

I don't want to be a "Like" someone,

I want to tell my own story.

I Can Breathe Fire Too!

~

I can breathe fire too!

I can say the hateful, cruel things you do,

I can spit acid from the tongue,

inject venom with my teeth,

as I dig them in, deeper to your throat,

I too, can bite the hands that feed!

I can burn bridges, sow salt across the land,

but...I won't, yet you will never understand,

I'm not like you, I can't pretend,

I can only be myself, don't you understand?!

Feral Whippings

~

Forced into nature,

claw marks sink into my side,

duel with the wolfs,

defend the women from the bears,

exile of humankind,

tear into the festered carcass of deer remains,

take what I can to survive,

locked back up into cages,

beaten into submission,

docile is the fervor look in my blazing eyes,

chain this savage beast,

snarling when your arm tries to reach,

I need not the helping hand,

I don't need this feed you offer me,

a petting zoo turned into a hunting ground,

kill or be killed, eat or be eaten,

I need to feel the wind,

the touch of dirt and grass upon my knees,

bare, dirt ridden feet,

tap across the roots of trees,

into the wild I was aborted to,

toes for claws, helps rip away the meat,

elongated incisors catch the fish in streams

instinct is blood, blood is like water,

life is wake up and sleep, kill and then feast,

life is simple until you eye up the prey,

blood crazed and starved enough,

to silence the neighing,

the crying of the newborn fawn,

will you sympathize and starve,

or survive tonight and see the dawn?

Flesh of the Gods

~

If there was a source of immortality,

we would all taste it,

yet I believe we would spit it out,

or regurgitate it,

I know it would taste bitter-sweet,

upon the tongue,

when one would live forever,

and all around them,

would perish into the never.

Some claimed to have tasted it,

some say they can describe it,

the texture, the smell,

and the sensation it gives within,

it soothes the soul, yet dries the mouth,

from a thirst that is never quenched,

and a growl in the stomach,

from the hunger left unsatisfied,

and if one claims to have taken a sip,

from the fountains of youth,

swam in the rivers of gold,

I beseech you, no I humor you,

cut their flesh,

and see if it bleeds,

I bet it will…

The Coliseum

Intro.

The Man in the Arena

~

"It is not the critic who counts;

not the man who points out how,

the strong man stumbles,

or where the doer of deeds,

could have done them better.

The credit belongs to the man,

who is actually in the arena,

whose face is marred,

by dust and sweat and blood;

who strives valiantly; who errs,

who comes short again and again,

because there is no effort,

without error and shortcoming;

but who does actually strive to do the deeds;

who knows great enthusiasms,

the great devotions;

who spends himself in a worthy cause;

who at the best knows in the end,

the triumph of high achievement,

and who at the worst,

if he fails, at least fails while daring greatly,

so that his place shall never be,

with those cold and timid souls,

who neither know victory nor defeat..."

The Coliseum
Part. I
The Offering

~

I stand there naked,

under shadows and blistered heat,

the crowds roar on the other side of the gate,

I'll feed the lions,

blood upon my enemies sword,

just they wait, just give me a weapon,

I'll fight back, I'll show them pain and scorn,

I need no armor, I've lost my faith,

I am one man against a legion,

I am one man taken a slave,

I am one man, I must not lose courage,

I must be determined, I must be brave,

an offering to the gods,

for the blood will run red today,

in the arena, where the offering will be made,

my blood to drink, my blood to induce,

bacchanalia will end the festivities,

while my heart beats in the lions stomach,

and the teeth tears at my bones,

getting what meat they can from my starved body,

but I'll strike back, I'll make them pay,

within an arena of many, there will be only one,

it will be I who is last standing over those I slay!

The Coliseum
Part. II
Never Surrender

~

Cornered, blood drips down my shoulders,

half my scalp ripped away,

lion claws tattoo my back and shoulders,

gladiator blades stab me,

I've been disarmed, I've been put on display,

put into a corner, and the enemy closes in,

my blade is gone, only my fists I bear,

but the cuts are deep, they bleed, the skin tears,

life drips away from me, surroundings blacken,

I lunge forward with my fists,

shoved back into the corner, nowhere to go,

I have no armor, I have no weapon,

I am a man who's lost to an empire,

a man put on display, to be a sacrifice to the emperor,

I am one man, whose strength is waning,

one man whose life is failing,

one man who has no calling,

for this is the end, and death is the beginning,

let it be known, that this man here today,

he did not die in vain,

he did not waste the courage that should have strayed,

he stood up to the impossible,

he fought the odds placed in front of him,

they may hit harder, but I carry a will stronger,

they may carry unity, but I carry honor,

for they hide among numbers,

I face this danger alone and on my own,

as I die in this corner with nowhere to go,

with the beasts that bite, and the claws that tear,

the centurions throw the net around me,

and drag me out to the middle of the coliseum,

they kick me while I'm down,

throw the dirt in my face,

they cut, they rip, the lion roars in triumph,

the gladiators raise their arms in victory,

the crowds roar, a standing ovation,

and the time has come, the final decision,

they call for blood, they call for slaughter,

thumbs held down to hell,

pointing south, the suspense is held,

all eyes are on the one, the god,

the emperor of the many, the leader,

the purveyor, to bring them,

entertainment and pleasure,

the son of the gods, the chosen of divinity,

the all-powerful, the all-knowing,

he looks to them, then down upon me,

he may do what he will, I spit at thee,

I'm kicked, they bleed me,

for showing ignorance to their master,

for disrespecting their noble cause,

oh how I wish to live on,

only to see this empire crumble,

see the walls fall all around,

crush the people, slay their leaders,

and when there is nothing left,

they eat each other,

they feast upon the weak,

and then the emperor is full,

filled by the flesh of his royal subjects,

and then the lions gather round,

and tear apart this bloated, spoiled man,

eat this glutton pound per pound,

he knows this, he sees it in my eyes,

if I live to stay a slave, if I do not die,

I will escape, you mark my words,

I will get away, I will find a way,

the emperor and his dominion, I will slay,

I am a threat to his entire civilization,

and so the decision has been made,

and my judgment, the thumbs are down,

and I lay here in pain, face to face,

with my fate, beaten and battered into nothing,

they took it all, they took it all away,

except for one thing, there is one important factor,

one thing I will never surrender,

they took my body, they take my life,

but they never took me, they never broke me,

I never gave up,

I fought down to the very last,

me, myself, and I,

an army of me versus an entire legion,

but I did it, I have won,

I may have ended up on the bottom,

but in principal, and for what it matters,

I am still who I am,

I am still on top,

I can say, as the final blow is about to strike,

I take my last breath, and I cry out loud,

"I never gave up! I die proud...for none of you,

broke my pride, you cannot break my spirit,

I die a hero today, a sacrifice for others to follow,

to learn a lesson, on what it means,

to stick to what is important, and never give in,

be your own...and never give in...!"

And the sun, fades like a swollen eye,

behind the clouds, out of sight,

I just want to see the light...of this perfect day,

see that gorgeous sky,

one last time...before I...

before I...a faint light....

shines...through...hope...

is shining...through....

Tiresias

~

"Bring forth the ram..." said the prophet,

toss it into the flames,

let the fire scorch the flesh,

let the underworld have its soul,

for your path is before you,

it's all been laid out for you hasn't it?

You know your doom, but not the hour,

you know...where you must go,

oh mighty king,

you know where this quest must lead,

don't worry, for I shall send word to your family,

to Ithaca, the head of the messenger,

upon black harpy wings,

you see it can't you?

within the swirling pool of your thoughts and mind,

you know...where your destination lies!

You have been forewarned,

by the goddess Circe that came before,

for it is her children, her spawn,

that you must come face to face...

"She lurks in the dark,

Scylla, a beautiful nymph once,

her many heads, a ring of barking dogs,

they will hear you, she will smell you,

they will awaken her,

a right nasty bitch from her slumber,

seven headed serpent of dread,

these women of the dark,

will reach out from beyond darkness,

craving human flesh, she will snap and bite,

and take your men...one by one...

and digest them in the night,

they will sleep in her guts, in pieces...!"

"Tidal pool Charybdis,

she invites you in with her luring call,

her sirens song pulsates up from the sea floor,

her echoing gut screams for blood upon her gaping lips,

and once you realize you've come to close,

there will be no escape from her pull,

her whirlpool will never let you go

as you and all your men are swallowed whole...!"

And Tiresias grasps Ulysses by the arm,

the decrepit old man squeezes tight,

as the hero looks into those empty white pools,

of the prophet's blind eyes,

that's when he realizes,

his time in the underworld is about to expire...

"You can run King Ulysses,

but pace yourself,

for when you come face to face,

with the accursed spawn of Circe,

that's when you will come to realize,

you will see that the path laid out for you,

is to spend your afterlife in the underworld,

for all eternity...!"

And the fading laughter of Tiresias,

is now behind him, echoing in the halls of Pluto,

as Ulysses climbs the rocks,

and severed crags, takes the ebony steps,

back up to the surface,

where he will feel daylight again...

Titan

~

Tearing your mortal corpse apart,

limb from limb,

make a pig of myself,

and gorge the flesh from your bones,

devour your race and consume,

the slaughtered herd of sheep,

your sacrifice to my immortal being,

devour and eradicate your wasted souls,

then regurgitate your futile flesh!

Gargantuan beast that casts his wrath,

upon the earth,

and destroys and deteriorates,

the sheer memory of a place called home,

I rule this universe by the hands,

soaked in the blood of the Olympian Gods!

I am the constructor of mortal pain,

I am the fire that burns,

the intestines in the stomach of the earth,

I am the cosmic monstrosity,

all terror that is disdain,

I am the titan, and dominance,

over the realms of flesh and blood,

is what I crave!

Burning your placid lands,

down into boiling seas of flame,

I demand a sacrifice of mortal blood,

in my dog-spawned name,

bury your diseased and masticated bodies,

in ruins and ashes,

of all that you have accomplished,

all that you conquered is now mine,

worship my dominance and herd,

more butchered lambs for me to feast,

fail to obey my tyranny,

and I shall splatter your guts,

throughout eternity!

Devour my children,

from the gaping womb of the earth,

to avoid certain prognosis,

the castration of my power,

decapitation of my diadem of blood and souls,

defile my hands,

with the crimson tides of your annihilation!

I am the constructor of human pain,

mold your veins into humans of clay,

then crush your bones,

and the let the rubble blow away,

I am the polar acid,

that deteriorates the skin of the earth,

I am the universal emperor,

of power who's rule is disdain,

I am the titan, and my rule shall forever remain!

Blood Star

~

Most wish upon a star,

they follow the North Star to their destination,

but I call upon the instrument of annihilation,

the sacred blood star,

the ripper of the flesh,

the terror of mortality,

once its granted access to this world,

it will never be removed,

once I make the cut deep into you,

the sacrifice is done,

the blood star is now in my possession,

and there is nothing anyone can do.

The immortals are taken apart,

the titans have been brought down,

I disembowel them,

for the pieces and parts I need,

I shape the veins into flaming blades,

the muscle becomes the basis for all torture,

and the star takes form,

tissue is welded,

the seams of convulsions and arteries,

have been sealed, it's only a matter of time,

until I wield my weapon of choice,

no sword neither shield,

no gun or firearm,

can protect against the destruction,

of the blood star.

No wall, no castle,

no fortress, no mountain,

can protect from the blood star's eradication,

once it chews into bone,

there is no satisfaction to its hunger,

once it gets a taste of you,

it will seek, forever and ever,

it will never stop, it must find,

for when I cast this weapon,

it will hunt you down, it will not stop,

until it consumes you...

An Angel's Snow

~

A resurrection, alive again,

a bloody nose drips upon white-hot sand,

holy ecstasy, thy I shall consume,

a snort per day, how much more can I do?

Two or three by noon, how much more,

until I'm through.

"...collapse, the angel's call soothes...

...I see the light that waits beyond sight..."

A resurrection, alive again,

a steel sword stabs my heart,

an incarnation, am I born again?

"Out to the Edge..."

~

"I walk...I walk up this somber hill,

I look across the still waters, and I feel...empty,

there I see, it stands before me...

a somber, opaque monolith,

an idol standing still. And the chill it brings,

is a numbing wind with no feel..."

I.D.O.L

~

An empty awakening,

from a slumber without sleep,

too many bad tastes on the tongue,

so many offerings you have eaten,

escapades under a neon glow,

the makeup is perfect,

yet your ugliness underneath always shows,

stage lights and bratty demands,

brighten the eyes,

the sweetness in a smile can disguise,

never give back, what's handed to you,

accept the praise, and give empty "thank-you's",

ignorance is blissful,

when no memories bring happiness,

and no company relates,

and the closest despise and hate,

deny all family who try to help,

who place their offering at your feet,

obey your own volition's,

accept the blood and drink of the weak,

let the dying pass,

pay no heed to the vigil they keep bedside,

but they will still die,

the families will still weep,

yet you'll live on,

immortality is only the beginning,

you want the eyes, the attention,

the fortune and the fame,

the money to bring more satisfaction,

never sharing, never ashamed,

the focus of your universe,

the sun that shines,

the lightning that keeps striking,

scorch your flesh, the crust of your earth,

with cigarette burns, and drown your sorrows,

in rivers of wine, and spiral downwards,

over the falls of tomorrow,

snort the future through your nose,

and your world sparkles,

your life as a living idol,

wouldn't perfection be so divine?

The weak and crippled will never walk or run,

the sick and dying will never recover,

never live on,

the standard of living declines,

while your exploits will blossom,

when another petal falls,

your weeds will flourish,

you have it all, when others have none,

and give you what little they still hold onto,

and you'll get more...won't you? You'll get it all!

Never satisfied, never full,

ignorance is blissful,

deny those who want true love,

obey the violence,

attack the slander and blasphemy

the gossip in thy name,

let the weak get trampled in the herd,

as the idiots flock to your worship,

to bow before you,

and praise the empty monolith,

the blank and empty deity that you really are,

ignorance is your moniker,

denying your followers truth is your practice,

obeying is what you expect,

life is yours to be had,

and deny all others their chance to live,

is to them your gift, what you pass,

empty calories for them to indulge,

why should they follow you? Tell me, please!

Why should they worship you?

Why should any get down on their knees?!

Why praise relics from the past,

and give them precedence,

in a future come to pass?

When it's you we don't need!

When we bleed,

we bleed into that empty, wooden bowl,

and then you'll drink, every last drop,

your cup have runneth over,

your no messiah, your hands don't heal,

how can you give value,

when behind turned backs you steal,

your time is up,

OD from a lifetime of selfishness,

now your eternity is on the line,

you'll feel the crippling pressure,

you'll feel the deaths of many,

you'll hear the dying screams,

you'll feel the scratch from the claws of reality,

when it's behind bars you'll be the bitch,

or buried six feet in a makeshift ditch,

for now you're the one that's screaming for help,

and everywhere you turn,

your followers, your friends,

your family, all gone...no one is there,

no one cares,

isn't life a bitch, this is what you get in return,

doesn't mortal pain hurt,

or is it karma getting it's vengeance,

lived your life in excess,

the more you ate, the less you have left,

it's all gone now, you swallowed it all away,

what's left upon your altar,

nothing but the empty sounds,

silent words from no followers,

the blank slate, the nothing,

you see that reflection in the mirror,

what is it you see? Go on, tell me!

I bet I can guess, it's nothing!

Inside of you, there's nothing.

On the outside and all around you, is nothing,

denial is a painful road to take,

left with nothing...you have fallen,

crumbled into fragments,

pieces that can never be put back together,

you will never be the same,

all the kings horses, and all the kings men,

will never put you back together again,

and forever these pieces will blow,

in the winds like dust, ashes to ashes,

trickle down the hill, penny for your thoughts,

before their taken from your eyes?

The pieces will be sprinkled,

over forgotten shores,

as they sink to the bottom of a cold, still lake,

if only you could go back,

and fix all those mistakes,

make amends, but there's one problem,

it's too late...

The Cosmic

~

Between every world, there is the connector,

the gate keeper, there is the doorway,

and at the doorway, there is the cosmic,

the vast and endless space, the connection,

and the connection lies within one,

a chosen of the higher planes,

beyond the realms unseen,

and for this world,

the connector to that other side,

to hold the hands of those that go on seeking,

an odyssey of undreamed of meaning,

and forgotten time,

where the ancient societies go on existing,

that cosmic,

the connection to this world and the next,

is me, so take my hands and you will see,

an undreamed of time lost beyond all infinity,

I'll take you to that place that should not be.....

Children to the Universe

~

Without the stars, I could never see,

the vast space and time,

where all begins, and the ever won't end.

And the smooth, ageless hands of divinity,

reach out, never reaching,

never gripping, all those lights,

all those eyes that shine,

spotlights to all those realms,

beyond all our kind.

Nestled in their systems,

a framework to build,

and protect individual existence,

the provider of the elements,

the mother of the balance,

keeps us in our space,

our own special corner,

where our existence is kept safe.

A Butterfly's Wing

~

And I see lying there,

a butterfly's wing,

and I know, she was a living, breathing thing,

I wonder however, if she ever had a song to sing?

Did she realize what fate would bring?

Was her wing left there for me to find,

by some fate, is there meaning?

What is the story behind this butterfly's wing?

Of Chaos & Doom...

~

Nothing much going on this evening,

just me and my friend,

walking under dying sunlight,

passing under molten stars waning,

we like to travel through time to places,

as we walk along our favorite road,

a nighttime's worth of spaces,

carved from shadowed earth,

as we traverse into eternal night together,

we don't look back,

as the trees and bushes swallow us whole,

we have no home,

we build a new citadel as we go,

we traverse lands where the light doesn't glow,

we arrive at dusk,

and part before the sun is shone,

so onward my friend, the road is long and old,

let's keep one step ahead of the dawn in bloom,

and keep to the land as shadows,

just me, Chaos...

and my friend who I call Doom.

Under an Autumn Moon

~

I feel the cold wind brush against my face,

for the crisp leaves,

of a dying holiday have come to pass,

as we trample through the woods,

across dead grass.

Far atop the hill,

just beyond the tombstones and mausoleums,

beneath a gray sky,

under an autumn moon,

blood is spilled in the pagan ritual,

as adept druids chant to the sacred runes,

of Wolf, the howl of the feral beast,

of Tree, enticement and entangled

by lust under the sacrificial knife,

of Wind, the breath of the goddess,

scrapes the cold soil due east,

of Fire, ignite the flame and burn this heretic,

spill this holy blood,

and on the flesh we will feast,

as I a man, and you a woman,

transform into lusting beasts,

for deep within, our inner spell is unleashed.

The Cat

~

The cat went to play,

in the graveyard today,

her master called,

and she obeyed.

The cat went to lay,

by her owner's grave,

she heard the whisper,

and she obeyed.

The cat went to stay,

spend the night by her master's grave,

and wait for his soul to rise,

when the devil comes to take him away.

The cat went to weep,

where the body of her master sleeps,

for when the devil comes,

the cat prays for his soul to keep.

The cat went to play,

in the graveyard today,

she's heard her master's plea,

as his body rises from the grave.

The cat went to lay,

by her owner's grave,

but the grave was empty,

the devil has come, and taken master away.

The cat didn't come to the graveyard today,

all she hears is the echo of an empty grave,

for the legions of hell, took the master away,

there is no crying over, an unhallowed grave.

The devil has taken her master away,

the cat will not return, she's moved on,

as time passed by, she no longer cries,

she's forgotten why her master went away.

The cat forgot that when, the master gave her life,

he placed the soul of his love,

the essence of his wife,

into the form of a cat, so they could be together.

His wife forgot,

that when he gave her a second chance,

the master sold his soul, to the devil as a slave,

and when you bargain with the devil,

it's your soul to pay...

Creepher

~

"Keep close child,

and don't you blink,

you see that scary person out there,

it's looking at you I think.

It will not go away,

it might be evil I think,

it's smile sinister,

or maybe it's laughing,

daring you, my child,

to come and play..."

SEESAW

~

See saw cut,

see saw grind,

see saw tear into your spine.

Hear saw rip,

hear saw shred,

the saw will not cease, until you're dead.

Smell blood on the saw,

smell smoke from cutting through bone,

your name is on the butcher's list,

and you're not alone.

The saw carves the meat,

the saw chews the flesh,

cadavers hit the floor in pieces,

a gory, bloody mess.

The saw is genocide,

the saw is annihilation,

the saw will bring about human extinction.

See saw dice, see saw splay,

see guts splatter and veins get ripped away,

let's cut open the ribs and see what's on display!

Libretto for a Wolv
Pt. III
Eradication
~

Tied to the fate of this wasteland,

the keeper of the dead, the pile of bodies,

that lay slaughtered at my feet,

blood has been spilled once again,

shades of red, flesh torn like rags,

rays of light from the full moon,

fill my soul, cleanse my wounds,

have turned me into the shape of what I am,

the true face, of an altered half-breed,

the true entity that lays beneath,

reveal to these people, the true face of the beast!

Face to face, with the machinegun men,

blades of silver gripped in their hands,

army fatigues and battle ready,

about to undo my curse, about to end my reign,

cleanse the terror of the wolf man,

a horror, a disease, a beast that lives to only feast,

take my life, and pierce the crest, dig in deep,

and tear out the heart from my chest,

skin the animal to reveal a man,

a cursed man, who bears the mark upon his hand,

a gift from the she-wolf, that keeps this man,

from living as a simple man, walks at night turned,

a complex cycle of walking among man as beast,

and beast as man, the final cry of the wolf,

howl to the moon, this is my final stand,

hold me back, from my one true love,

I love her too much, to lust for her blood,

see her tears, at the scene of this crime,

what have I done? Drank the blood of the innocent,

the man inside she loved has died.

Hunched back and ready, I pounce,

I hold my claws up high, ready to attack,

a snarl echoing across the sky,

and that's when the bullets fly,

silver bursts, bright sparks flash before my eyes,

machinegun fire at the strike of the midnight chime,

blood splatters, fur is torn away,

the flesh of the beast has been pierced,

no corner to crawl to, to lick my wounds clean,

and all ceasefire, and all goes quiet, except for a moan,

and the screams and cries of my love held behind enemy lines,

a final howl, of the wolf king who hath fallen from his throne,

a final dance, a celebration in quartet and arpeggio,

set the stage for the last chapter, the climax is my final libretto,

I howl to the crowds, I howl to the sky,

beyond all heavens, beyond all time,

I howl till my soul reaches the final line, a higher realm,

beyond my flesh, beyond my crimes,

a realm that will claim the man that is left behind,

I howl with all my strength, of all that is left within me,

I howl to the earth, as death begins to take me,

and hell echoes back, and my howl wanes down,

as my dying body collapses, the seven bells ring,

the bells from the church steeple chime,

and the last day of summer has died,

the season is over, and the full-moon wanes,

the leaves fall, as all life passes by,

as my life passes before me, as the man in black,

sickle by his side, puts the muzzle and the leash upon me,

ready to escort me, the soul of a savage animal,

to his afterlife beyond infinity, a cage of silver to confine me,

the silver courses through my blood, the silver nectar,

an allergy, a vile affliction upon the beast in me,

the wolf reverts back, to the tell-tale signs of a forgotten face,

the face of a person my true love once kissed,

when our bodies embraced, when she recognized and loved,

this man before he became a walking abomination,

a monster in the eyes of the human race.

She rushes forward, and holds me in her grasp,

stares into the monster's faded eyes,

as my eyes, she can recognize, she sees past the beast,

and can see the man,

a tear drop rolls off her cheek, as she prays for my soul,

to find the eternal rest I seek.

The lush coat of this beast starts to fade,

and the flesh is exposed, the beast becomes a man,

the fangs morph into teeth, I smile at that pretty face,

I love this woman deeply, and I hope she can see,

the smile of me, the man I used to be,

my claws become hands, the hands she would hold,

the hands of her man, not the claws of a butcher,

responsible for so many deaths at this monster's grasp,

its slash and thrash, its chewing and tearing,

its biting and lapping, the crowds are cheering and clapping,

my death brings them salvation, for I am the last,

and with my death, my species faces eradication,

for no more blood, shall stain the earth,

no more shall a death of my doing, be discovered,

for this beast has been slain, all that's left,

is the final breath of a restored man,

restored, yet will never walk this earth again,

for I shall pass beyond the realms of time and space,

where will I go, what will be my fate?

I fear because of what this beast has done...for redemption,

it is far too late. Enough blood has been spilled,

and there is no need to retaliate,

all I ask, in this...my final line, my ultimate end,

is to look upon her...one last time...

to my love, to see that purest look within her eyes,

I say goodbye to you...my dearest...my bride,

this is the end of the cycle for me...

my time amongst mankind has reached the end of the line,

as the man you once loved, I say to you with his final words,

goodbye my love...good...bye...

And the seven bells ring,

the angel of death sings,

"..oh, what shall be done,

what judgment can be brought upon...

the tortured spirit, of a malicious beast,

who shares the same body,

with a cursed man, whose soul may rest in peace?

Oh woe is me...who must bring judgment upon,

one man and one beast, yet this beast is now the man,

a killer of man by instinct,

and the man...shared his heart with this beast...

the beast, man sought out and killed,

is this a man, or is this a beast?!"

Libretto for a Wolv

Pt. IV

Rebirth

~

(...thud thud...thud thud...thud thud...)

you hear the heart beat?

That's the sound of a new beginning,

a cycle never ending,

for the song of the wolf,

the howl of the lycanthrope,

will echo for eternity...

(...thud thud...thud thud...thud thud...)

echoes the fetus,

of the prenatal wolf-child,

the hybrid that grows inside her belly...

For I cannot die, my curse will live on,

my child will soon be born,

and reign as a king in the wild,

but must be a peasant among the humans,

for this plague of immortality,

that I spread, must be kept a secret,

for not even the mother can understand,

the cycle of beast and human,

the chronicle of war, the battle between,

two opposing forces, two beasts that stand,

forever rages on, the battle,

of wolf and man,

and still I ask the question,

still this question stands,

is the transformation from man to wolf,

in reality wolf to man...?

In a land without Giants

~

We used to scuttle, we used to crawl,

scavengers under those that were big and tall,

the giants who ruled over one and all,

but no more do we fear them,

no more do we flee, no more do we run,

since the day they fell,

since the day their civilization crumbled,

and the tall ones, the big and loud came tumbling down,

smashed under their rubble,

just as they would smash us under their heels,

pluck off our wings, pull off our legs,

just to watch us scuttle, just to see us crawl,

just for fun, to see us flap around,

and then they would smash us, they would squash us,

our desiccated bodies left forgotten at the bottom,

swept into corners, a dust pan to carry us to our burial,

emptied into the bottom of the trash can,

our bodies pile up, lives taken for granted,

our tiny lives have been wasted,

but now they're gone, and we're free to move around,

no longer are we bound to holes,

no longer do we breed in our caves,

as we rise up and repopulate the earth,

as we scuttle across the remains of their skulls,

buried in the dirt.

The Final Day

~

The final days have come, repent...repent,

read the sign of the walking man,

bring out your dead, the bell ringer chants,

as bodies all around are gathered,

to be fed into the burning pit,

by men in gas-masks,

machine-guns on their backs,

holy men gather their mass,

to say a final prayer, a final word of fear,

a word of despair, a word of suffering

crosses around their necks,

devils and angels at war behind their backs,

prepare for judgment,

for doom is almost near,

the time will come,

when we rise from our graves,

and join the legions,

of the flesh-eating dead,

the blood suckers that only come out,

at the stroke of midnight,

the end is nigh,

for the signs are all too clear,

Armageddon is almost here,

the end of times draws near,

read the sign upon the homeless man,

the walking dead, the prophet said,

he carves the cross into his head,

to protect himself from being damned,

he knows it's all too clear,

heed his warning,

he knows the final day is near.

Storm of Steel

~

Before you go,

just remember my name,

even if I have to burn it into,

your flesh, to stick to your mind,

even a tattoo is not permanent,

but that scar upon your skin,

from my laser eyes,

from the acid in my mouth,

will stand the testament of time,

you won't forget,

that's not a promise,

I ask you nothing,

it's a fact, it's a command,

for a fact is demanded,

a force unlike any natural disaster,

you cannot stop it,

can you feel it?

You cannot run from it,

try to...go on and run,

I'll grab the sun and bleed it dry,

extinguish the light,

the sight from your eyes,

the reflection of colors in your mind,

the warm air on your skin,

has been replaced by a burn,

a sting you will feel,

when you roll over in bed,

when you put on your shirt in the morning,

the soap in the shower will scold it,

the blood it drips will spread it,

the scar I carved will preserve it!

That memory will always be there,

that little nuisance,

is it an inconvenience?

Good, because now I know,

you'll never forget,

you'll always remember my name,

cut deep into your skin,

when you dared to cross my line,

dared to break me down,

dared to salt my wounds when I was down,

you never thought I would fight back,

you thought I'd just walk away,

you thought I was worthless,

that I could not feel,

and now you'll never forget,

that you better not fuck with a bitter man,

at the center of his storm,

a raging storm of steel...

Nightlepers

~

Twisted women, faces under silk shrouds,

milky white skin, bumps and sickness,

famine absorbed the bastards,

plague has killed the fathers,

and these people wander restless,

and the disease spreads without reasons, aimless,

no more do the gutted bowls of the slaves panic,

for they sleep next to familiar faces,

faces of the rotting corpses,

of loved ones...of dead ones,

haunted sleep, restless sleep,

sickened dreams, famine of dead seeds,

planted eons ago, but to never grow,

starved victims to never feast,

restless victims to never sleep,

rotting flesh seeps, sagging eyes are blind,

open wounds bleed, and these lepers,

these lepers wander for eternity,

with a barrier between them and the living,

the undead of a community,

a community that leaves them be,

cast them away, never to be,

exist in the shadows,

never to be, and these lepers,

these lepers walk,

until it's time to sleep,

and these lepers crawl,

while sadness takes them,

for a second chance at life they weep,

and these lepers stagger,

these lepers sway,

they sit down and look at a sunset,

a sunset that darkens upon their time,

a time when they need the day,

and these lepers lay their head backs,

the muscle has rotted away,

the civilization has crumbled away,

and no more do they stand,

no more do they walk, no more does infinity call,

for the day has gone away, and at night,

at night...oh the wind cools the pain,

the night air seals them away,

the shadows keep them,

as the final stages of the flesh rot away,

as we pushed them away,

no more do they wander,

for by the fires they lay,

upon piles of the rotting they lay,

and the fire, the flames burn them away,

it's a shame, for I remember the night,

the night when we sent the lepers away,

all they wanted was our help,

all they wanted was to not die alone,

as this sickness took them away,

but that's what we did,

are we no better,

than a living necrotic condition?

That humans would turn away humans,

rather than help them?

As a disease would take them in,

and accept them?

Imaginary Friend

~

I talk to my friend all day,

you refuse to believe me, but he's here I say!

I talked to my friend yesterday,

Where did he go?

He only said…that tonight *"…you're gonna pay!"*

I guess you made him mad…

The Failed Creation

~

Womburned--born of mixed blood,

the newborn who suckles upon black milk,

bile spilled from the mother's breast,

the scars in life shall never heal,

speak words that are poison,

from your forked-tongue, the insults kill,

never to love, that is your fate,

only to beat, breed, and procreate,

failure in life has been branded and sealed,

when your mother found out she was late,

what you would gain from a hug or a kiss,

is a feeling that you will never experience,

people will keep pushing you and shoving you away,

to be alone inside, the bearer of dissonance for life to sing,

as that heart becomes clogged,

and then bandage the scars with cigarettes and liquor,

flesh that crawls like a million rancid spiders,

skin molten like fire, scales of an slimy worm,

bear your father's horrid image,

and carry the curse of your mother's heritage,

your breed will be scum,

your offspring parasites to feast upon others,

parentage is nothing more than a cast-down,

throw your children to the hounds,

and make them eat from the garbage,

guaranteed to rob others, to salvage what was never given,

so let's just end this here and watch you struggle,

watch you try to swim,

keep your premature, bastard-child head afloat,

in a rising sea of desperation,

that will not stop until you're tired,

and you and all your own, are swept away,

upon the waves, as life drags you under...

Homecoming...

~

"He's coming home again,

to take your hand,

and play games of just pretend,

the forgotten son, the chosen one,

he'll show you the way to the promised land..."

Dark Sun

~

It's only a matter of time,

till the wick rekindles,

the cannons fire, heed the warning,

the stars align to show him the way,

the pieces have moved, checkmate confines,

in that peaceful atlas of his mind,

now disturbed, for it is time,

maps of destiny falter his reality,

his path has strayed, he lost his way,

it was our own doing, we created a monster,

and now...we must pay.

Where there is no solace, no conformity,

stagnant throughout the wild wind,

in his mind that roars like a tornado,

storms of his past, come back to destroy,

villages and cities shall fall,

civilizations will crumble,

cool air upon the hair of this wolf's chin,

time stands still in this bitter man,

we're just pigs to the butcher man,

a sacrifice of bahhhing, frightened lambs.

"He's coming home again, do you remember,

the last time he was in town?

when we tortured him, made fun of him,

burned his house down, poisoned his dog,

violated his mom, harassed him,

tore into him, like removing stuffing from a doll,

we took everything, even his sister's virginity,

we did it all, we took it all from him,

the scars were so deep...if only we knew,

but in a sick twist, I think we did,

oh the sick, vile things we did,

to strike a nerve, to hear this pathetic boy weep,

fantasize about the pain he feels in his sleep,

if we only could sympathize,

if we could have known, the pain he felt,

if we could relate, but we would only decimate,

we had our fun, it was teenage joy,

this piss-poor kid, he was just a toy,

we moved on, we never looked back,

but now, the time has come,

he's come back, a shadow arisen,

from our intoxicated past."

"He's come back to claim his kingdom,

to dip his crown in our blood,

rip our flesh apart with the machine gun,

tip the scales of balance, and get even,

we were the ones, we were the heathens,

the fate of a king we called a clown,

he smiles, and we all frown,

he pulls the gun, the razor, the fire,

hang us up, crucified one by one,

the blood runs to our heads,

pointed at the ground,

we try to run, we try to flee,

and we all fall down,

the darkness in this poor man's history,

we were young boys, we were hateful kids,

we can never be forgiven for the things we did,

if only we knew...the tragic life,

the dark son had to live..."

Tower of Shadows

~

There it sits on a hill and watches,

a hill of ash and death,

that poisons with each breath,

and blinds with each stare.

Its gaze is a never-ending shadowy night,

with steeples that cry in agony and despair,

with the thunder of its unhallowed bells,

ringing in the midnight air.

It's walls are trimmed,

with the dark reflections of its past,

the grim story of its own construction,

its ancient spires and bricks however,

will crumble to its own self-destruction.

Invisible with the night,

whilst the day fades away with its hue,

innocence cries in terror,

when its chant rings through.

The shadow is once more calling,

its paralyzing touch cannot be removed,

the tower is crying out for you!

HIS grasp...cannot be removed!

Tormento 6:66

~

I. In His Name...

Sit around my fire children,

and heed these words I say,

for I am your friend,

you can trust in me,

for I shall not lead you astray.

Beware the light,

for it shall blind your path,

sit close to me, heed my whispers,

and I shall protect you,

within my darkness, you will feel comfort,

cradled by my shadow,

you will feel my warmth,

I will protect you from the false One's wrath...

II. THE GOAT KING

Be strong...be vigilant,

do not surrender to his temptation,

for when you meet the black king,

upon his golden throne,

he will offer you power,

he will offer you the world,

he will offer you the skeletal hand of love,

the lies of death wrapped in the flesh,

of a woman's silhouette,

as the bloody trident is raised at your back,

you are marked, you have been chosen,

branded by the baphomet,

five prongs, five diadems,

adorn the old goat's head,

and the Goat King's crown,

has been placed upon your brow,

you are the sons and the daughters,

the bastard children,

the whores and the liars,

all spawns of the deceiver,

the concubines to his will,

the disciples of his bidding,

you have chosen the path of night,

to stray from the protection,

and guidance of My light,

eternal bliss is unforgiving, for once it's decided,

eternal damnation, is yours by choosing,

you will not walk in my garden,

you shall not pass my gates,

my heavenly shower,

will not ascend thee upon your dying day,

you belong to the Goat King now,

and for your soul...only Hell awaits!

III. Sepphia's Chime

"Within the darkness...a dream so divine...."

Across the vast and endless seas she takes me,

I follow her heart, her heart that is the music,

the beat of love, that is her chime,

the light caress across the pipes,

and the winds carry her vocals,

so sweet...so divine,

the nectar of the vocals,

lays like sweet dew upon my ears,

with my lips...I can also taste the words,

I know her song when she plays,

I recognize her cries,

I am hypnotized by her lyrics,

for she had no words to speak...

only the sounds of heaven,

by her fingers as they strum,

her soul, her very essence calls to me,

her chimes play to beckon me,

to steer me through the darkness,

she leads me on my path across the waves,

she leads me to my destiny,

to where I need to be,

to be with her, my love...for all eternity!

I know now which way I must go,

for once I was lost,

but now I'm found,

I've found my way across this endless tide,

as she brings me to the shores of Paradise,

so we can once more be together,

and see our children,

our loved ones, our brethren,

that have passed on to the other side,

lulled to sleep, by Sepphia's chime,

but as Tobias, my brother once said,

for I can hear his voice too,

his judgment overcomes my mind.

He says:

"...that the Goat King is a real trickster,

he beckons to us with false images,

we play out as we want to in our heads,

we give life to those he has captured...

those who he keeps within his shadow land,

are those we keep most sacred,

the most precious lifetimes in our memories,

are you too one of them, brother?

Do you eager so much to follow her?

To abandon the light,

and spend eternity in misery,

have your wedding in the fire,

presided over by those unmourned,

by those the light has cast out,

do you abandon the light as well, dear brother?

Do you dare pull back her black veil,

and see what is underneath,

spend your honeymoon in the abyss,

and bear the spawns of chaos and insanity?

Are you one with the light, or a serpent,

a snake of the Goat King's tribulation?

Do you leave us, your brother,

your mother and father?

Your family for lifetimes.

Do you abandon true love,

for a harlot who left you,

and never looked back?

Never took a second thought,

at her decision to follow the night,

and abandon the warmth of one,

who loved her...don't forget,

she left the protection of the one and true light!

Is her song so powerful as to sail you through,

the most unforgiving sea?!

Would you take a step onto the shore...

and abandon all who you left,

on the other side of this dream,

would you brother?

Would you slay us with the ebony blade?

Stab us in our backs with the knife in the dark?

Just to see her...would you?

For beware the image of Paradise...

for it may not be what you see...

What is Paradise truly dear brother?

Except what we make of it,

just another interpretation in our head...

just another game,

for the old Goat King to play with,

for his chosen are his puppets,

and he the commandeer,

the agitator, the tempter, dear brother,

please...don't let him tempt you!"

And so I awaken in a cold sweat,

a chill brought on by the raging seas,

the seas of thoughts and nightmares I've had,

almost lost to my imaginings,

my dreams so sweet...I care not how dark,

because I could see her!

I...I could see her image,

carried upon the waves of her sweet song,

and so I lay back into my pool,

of sweat and wonder...

would I have taken...that one step?

IV. PUEDO `

There's a little town buried under time and sand,

where burned hands reach out for cool air,

and dry throats seek the solace,

of water in a glass,

burned feet want to walk upon soft,

emerald grass,

and live in a house of comfort,

instead of clay huts and stone ziggurats,

worn and tatter clothes,

they drape across their skeletal bodies,

unable to breath this stifling air,

their scalp peels flesh from no hair,

their society is famine, their economy is broken,

for they long to leave these miserable lands,

at the center of all creation,

take to the coastal ships and fishing vessels,

and ride upon the tides of waves, and sail,

let the salty winds take them so far away,

for on the other side, in Paradise,

a more...relaxing existence awaits,

the winds will take you too, if you so wish,

to bask in the shade, of evening trees,

and a fresh rain upon your face,

where the light doesn't burn,

the light is banned from this sacred place,

for this little town of mud and brick,

will soon bask in the shadows,

and no more insignia's of the One,

will stand upon the outwards facing chapel,

these people of the desert,

have sacrificed all comforts,

to burn and blind themselves,

in the light's protection,

if they wish,

to have their comfort and relaxation,

then all they have to do...

is redirect their dedication,

but for a lifetime of comforts,

is it worth the price of damnation?

V. Dreams Turn to Flames

And the darkness boils around me,

I can feel the screams and hear the torture,

these are just the dreams, yet the reality of it all,

is harsher.

"Alone came the old man,

a long snout peaked from under the hood,

he said his name was Mendes,

an old ghost from long ago,

an ancient who has seen the passing of history,

one who has witnessed the genocide of infinity.

Mendes walked upon all three,

two hooves and a cane in his left hand,

with his right, he performed the sacred blessing,

the baptism,

a benediction for I have brought the offering,

my eternal soul I would give...

just to see the land across the sea,

just to see her, to walk with her hand in hand,

just to walk upon the peaceful shores to feel,

what it's like to be free..."

And just to get there, just to see her once again,

I would give anything,

I would give up my being.

I stay within this dream for some time,

that is where I see her smiling,

daydreams bring upon the night, the lights dim,

and hours melt...and death makes its passing,

reaps the bodies, harvests the sick and dying,

yet I simply ignore the passing,

and the coming of the end, for closer I am,

yet I could care less, for in Paradise,

there is no decay, there is no famine,

there is only utopia,

and the familiar faces we bring,

to become one with our dearly departed,

and blossom like flowers into another Spring.

So, if you pardon me,

I'll keep dreaming for a while,

my mortal coil is now in Mendes's hands,

the fate I receive will hurt at first,

but just like any change,

after the passing of time,

we come to acceptance, we come to understand,

that in order to see a better ending to the story,

we must make that decision at the cross-roads,

as to which direction awaits the final glory,

and only when we choose, and take the chance,

only then can we continue with our story.

For what is it that I am leaving?

A burning waste,

the shifting sands and cracked earth?

No water for miles,

and a parched mouth that has been scorched,

and skinned alive!

I flake like the lizards,

and shed my mortal coil,

like the spiders exchanging skins,

for in order to walk on grass,

we must cross the fire,

for Paradise burns with a somber desire,

in order to reach the streams,

we must climb the mountains higher,

in order to reach Paradise,

we must burn with the fire,

if we want to reach Paradise,

we must suffer through hell,

and I hear the chimes ringing,

I hear the gong of the southern bell.

"Take my palm, and prick your finger,

paint your destiny within my grasp,

for I can make your wishes,

and desires come to pass.

All we need is a helping hand...

and that I can offer you,

I can bring seas to your shore,

I can provide the means,

to reach your destination,

and final will be your departure,

and eternal will last your arrival,

I demand no pressure upon you,

for I am here to only help,

I assist where I can, all you have to do...

is ask, just make a simple wish..."

Alas, he told me nothing is for free,

but I know what I must do,

I know what I must give,

a sacrifice it is, and I am ready to appeal,

I am ready to gaze upon the light,

the blinding lantern,

hanging by the hooks in the sky,

I am ready to squash the fire fly,

and take that path at the crossroad,

though torture and wrath I will endure,

I am ready for the risk,

and accept the consequences,

for I over see my own path now,

and let Mendes guide me through the darkness.

And the darkness subsides from me,

I no longer fear the torture, am I deaf,

for the screams have fell silent,

it was just a dream,

I leave my bed, and head outside,

and that's when I see the torture,

that's when I hear the screams,

that's when I realize,

that my dreams are nightmares,

and my fantasy... is a harsh reality,

for at the foot of the hill, at the gates of Puedo`,

there stands the ghost of Mendes,

now of flesh and blood as black as oil,

and by his side upon a chain, is a black goat.

And the fires and smoke rise higher,

for this is what happens when Hell crosses over,

he beckons to me, the hooves tap and patter,

as he walks over bodies,

as he steps across marble,

and tramples through,

puddles of blood and trough water,

the waters boil as he passes,

and the steam raises to the clouds,

he stops in front of me, and with weakened legs,

I fall, and kneel upon the ground.

"You called to me,

in your sacred somber snooze,

and I have heard your praise,

and now I have come to you!

You wish to see Paradise,

and follow in my wake,

good...this is good to hear,

for I have made your decision easier,

and burned your village and all you loved,

who would get in my way!

But...it's not these people you love in return,

oh no!

For you wish to see a lover,

a brighter light within your dreams,

and the more you praise to me,

she will be closer,

this bright light will only get brighter!"

My choice was so obvious, my choice was clear,

but now...something feels wrong,

and I feel the mists in my mind still linger.

He points off towards the left,

he motions towards the right,

and at all sides are nailed the bodies,

posted up as signs,

signs that are clear, signs I am forced to read,

my brother, my mother, and father...

are dead, and hang before me.

My tears sincere,

my conscious and life has been taken,

I have nothing more to lose,

and I look upon the old man,

I stare into those haunting, glowing red eyes,

I reach for the dead hunters spear,

and lunge it through the sky,

I look out to see if I made my mark,

yet to only see old Mendes kneeling over,

the body of the dead, black goat,

stuck by the hunter's spear,

and I have shown that Old Goat Man,

for my choice is all too clear,

I will not follow his darkness, and by the light,

I will face him!

By the light of the One, I will persevere!

Old Mendes spreads his wings,

and cloaks himself from attack,

weakened by the death of his pet,

I have landed a mortal blow,

and I will force my own way,

to Paradise, and see it burn,

a land of lies, a land for the spurned!

And when I come face to face,

with my love, with the light of my dreams,

I will do what I must,

and I will embrace her,

I will love her once more,

before I release her,

before I heal her, before I free her,

I will remove her head,

by the spear of the hunter,

cursed by the goats blood,

by the armor I will take from the temple,

of the sacred One,

I will brandish my sacred family cleaver!

And so, I ready myself,

and prepare for my quest to Paradise,

for my pilgrimage...my journey has begun!

I say to myself...I remember those words,

the words of the One...

VI. Words of the One

"...have faith and keep trust,

thy brothers and sisters,

thy sons and daughters,

for you may follow your heart,

you may follow your wants and desires,

to an end of your own choosing...

but I swear to all of ye,

who follow in the trail of HE,

those who've been marked,

those who are chosen,

will feel my light no more...

for once you gaze upon the realms of Paradise,

there will be no return for you,

for you now bask in the moon of him,

the him of many faces and many names,

the him who shelters in the darkness,

in the shadows of my light,

spell my name backwards,

and you will know the one I mean!

For if you chose to follow the Goat King,

I will have no remorse,

for my eyes will remain ignorant,

and your names...

those I call my brothers and sisters,

those who are my children faithful,

will have committed the ultimate betrayal,

and your names shall grace the list,

your exploits

shall be told in stories and hymns...

of Tormento 6:66!"

"May the One let me return,

for I go in his name,

to bring light to blind the dark,

and cleanse Paradise, burn the haunted land..."

And so I cross my heart, and hoist the sails,

to traverse the seas, and follow the winds shrill,

for Paradise calls, its song guides me,

I steer in the direction,

of the southern hemisphere,

and after three dawns and three dusks,

Paradise will be in sight,

it is then I realize, I take this quest alone,

to the land of seduction,

where the Goat King calls the lost home.

VII. CHOSEN

I am the chosen,

this task before me is mine, and mine alone,

I have been chosen,

to bring light to Paradise,

and let the darkness fade away,

for all eternity, banish the Goat King away,

I am the chosen one,

that is one, this task is my own,

I take the light of the One upon me,

and when this is all said and done,

if I live to see another dawn,

may the One, let me return home,

and if not, if I should pass,

into the shades of night,

if the shadows,

should swallow the rest of the light,

may the voices of my loved ones,

may their forgiven spirits guide me,

let them take me,

may their voices call me home...

But I have been chosen,

darkness lays in wait,

the trials that lay ahead of me,

may very well kill me,

that I am aware, that I understand,

and if it must, let it be,

let me die fighting, let me die,

waging the final war, between dawn and dusk,

day and night, moon and sun,

and if I'm successful, please...I beg of thee,

let it be so, let it all be over and done,

so that night, only consists of moon and star,

and the memory of the Goat King,

lies buried under the fires of Paradise,

dead and long gone, as time goes on,

let him stay deep, keep him asleep,

so that the remainder of the days,

never shed a tear, so that none may weep.

May the children sleep,

and let the dead rest in peace.

I have been chosen, to accept this quest,

I have been chosen,

to bear the weight of the world,

I have been chosen to end this plague,

lay these nightmares to rest,

and let the sleepless, have peace,

let those who become restless,

when the sun goes down,

let the restless sleep,

for I have been chosen,

and I accept my fate,

I will face what I must,

let me die, if that is to be, let it be,

but I will not think in such a way,

for I want to succeed,

to see the dawn of a new and coming Age,

I will be the catalyst, the foundation,

to build upon the next stage,

to rewrite history, and echo upon the lips,

of my descendants, when they tell my tales,

to their children, their grandchildren,

and their descendants will tell their own,

of what happened on this day,

the day our people won against the darkness,

the day that I slay the Goat King!

"...for once you gaze,

upon the realms of Paradise,

there will be no return for you..."

I beg thee, One who is light,

one who blinds the minions that hide,

within the wings, under the shadow,

of the Goat King's night, I beg thee,

I plead, I go in your name,

to punish the Goat King,

let me return...let me return,

let me return from across the sea,

I come here, not by the will,

of the Goat King...I come by my will,

to see his undoing,

to stop his lies from spreading,

I wish to return to the land of sunshine,

to a new... a better living,

where balance is restored,

and there is no more poverty,

no more suffering,

no more will you need to instill fear,

to keep us away from the Goat King.

If they call my name, I'll silence their tongues,

if they spill their lies, I'll spill their guts,

if they hunger for my essence, my very soul,

I'll drink of their blood, and swallow it all!

If happiness is pleasure, if happiness is paradise,

then I will suffer, suffer for the greater good,

suffer for the coming of a new Age,

I'll suffer for the rest of my days,

I'll die poor, I'll die alone,

I'll suffer till I'm old and gray,

I'll suffer for the greater good,

I'm ready to make my sacrifice,

I'm ready to save the day,

I'm ready to lead the down-trodden,

the forgotten, the cursed away,

give them one more chance,

let them find peace,

cleanse them of their mistakes,

let their faults be forgiven,

let us all be one again,

when the Goat King's influence,

has been washed away.

Promise me I can return to my home,

promise me my familiar land,

promise I can return to a new life,

a better relation with you, I chose you,

I follow you, I carry this light,

you gave to me,

I carry the spear, tipped in ram's blood,

I wear the armor of the light,

I wield the sword of my ancestors,

I carry my courage,

my courage will allow me to kill,

spill the blood upon Goat Hill,

where the throne of the Goat King,

will be revealed,

as the moon eclipses,

and light radiates from the sacred seas,

the tower arises over Paradise,

my way will be revealed to me,

I follow this path into darkness,

I follow this path to my fate,

I follow my heart upon this quest,

I will live or die as I may,

for I am the chosen,

I am the only one standing between,

eternal night, or a blissful day,

I ride this ship across the waves,

the island approaches, the tide carries me,

I near the beaches, within scope,

I can count every crag, every pebble,

along the shore, so lovely in the evening,

a liar underneath, the tidal waves carry me,

"...for once you gaze,

upon the realms of Paradise,

there will be no return for you..."

may the One release me...

or death...take me...!

VIII. On the Shores of Paradise

Bring me safe, to a remote and peaceful shore,

the shores of Paradise,

where the trees grow to the sky,

and the souls can hide within the shade,

I see her, I can see the paradise over there...on the horizon,

I can see Sepphia, my love, standing upon the sands,

waiting for me, singing her sweet song for me,

the goddess of love, blessed be her,

and that her soul will be at peace,

for she gives me light upon the shores of this dark place,

for the closer I near, the shadows curve over my head further,

and my love turns in the darkness,

feeble and bloated like a sick whore,

she's taken in too much splendor, she's given to much pleasure,

I thought I knew her...but now,

I can't recognize this sick, twisted tormentor,

it is as the one has said, *"She has become one with Corruptor"*,

she tries to hide her affliction,

but I can see right through those pale eyes,

I can hear the suffering beneath cracked lips unspoken,

for my eyes have awaken,

my voice calls to her,

to reassure her, that I will love her,

"I will spare her..."

for when her eyes shut, I shall miss their beauty,

and the star of Venus shall sprinkle her ashes,

in the dew drop of the morning,

and from my eyes the tears shall fall,

a drop of bitter salt, filled with the spice of mourning,

an ancient herb we once shared, we called it *"loving"*,

loving each other till the plant had died,

and we could not walk across the misty moors,

to collect its essence and drink of the sweet nectar we made,

"No more...no more will it be this way..."

"...for once you gaze,
upon the realms of Paradise,
there will be no return for you..."

"She cannot return...she cannot be healed...

she is too far gone, lost to the shadows of the Goat King,

sharing his bed, his wine, his kingdom...as his concubine..."

And in her decision...the One has banished her,

but I...I will love her once more...I will heal her,

at least she'll be at peace when death takes her.

And the boat touches the sands...the rocks and bones,

that materialize, for the illusion to fool,

can fool no longer, for I can see this paradise as it really is,

as what it doesn't seem,

a place of lies and manipulation, unloving...undying,

unsung are these lost souls without hope or reckoning,

of when the promises will be kept,

but they got what they paid for, freedoms to linger as slaves,

to the Goat King, roaming on fire,

their only light within this haze,

to suffer in torment as they scream, scream for help,

searching for the light they had lost, they lost their way,

searching for forgiveness,

of the Light they had turned away,

for the One has never forgiven,

none he ever forgave.

She holds out her hands, to welcome me,

for how long has it been,

since we last embraced,

months...days...years,

too many yesterdays, and not enough tomorrows,

there will be none, there will be only minutes,

there will be only this moment, this thread in time,

hand the knife to the fury, as she cuts the last thread,

of my love, I shall mourn her and the others,

of the damned who must join with the dead,

oh, the pain and torment, for I wish to stay,

for I wish to hold her,

to love the one I have loved for this brief life,

for what I thought would be forever,

but I no longer know her,

for I cannot love this...her,

I can only spare her.

"Come to me...my sweet,

bring to my lips your kiss,

for how long has it been,

since you had last kissed me..."

Her voice brings me...her eyes lure me,

I want her...oh how I want her,

but I cannot...this can no longer be!

I will not see her like this...

she is not a horrid creature in this place,

she does not deserve to be a slave,

hypnotized by the Goat King's poisoned words,

and deep, cold gaze,

I wrap my arms around her,

for one more moment, I will embrace her,

for that time must come,

when I must do, what I promised her,

I will love, what she once was, just this one last time,

then I must kill, this creature that lingers inside,

by spells that curse her, and ignorance that blinds her,

betrayal that scars her, by this love,

I will free her, I release her!

"A final kiss my dear, for this is not...

how I had seen forever, for now we must part,

only to see each other again,

in the ever-after, and maybe there can we make,

what we could not in life...may it be in death!"

She cannot understand these words I speak,

but I cannot speak no more, with a throat full of stutters,

and a mouth choking upon all my tears I shed for her,

as I drive the consecrated steel, into her chest,

as her fingers caress down my armor, as she falls to her knees, a trickle of blood drips from her mouth,

as she gasps...I can her that wheezing,

as she struggles to breathe,

and before me, the one I had loved,

is reappearing, becoming who she once was, my love,

the true form of the one I had loved,

for that hideous shell no longer consumes her,

she is free, and her arms cross, and eyes look up,

her head tilts, and left upon her lips...is what remains,

a reflection of her last word to me,

not a sound nor any guilt, but a smile,

for this is the lovely woman I know, the one I loved,

the woman who goes now to the heavens above,

across space and time, to where existence is forever,

may she be in peace...and when my time comes,

I will find her, and we will be together,

this I promise, this I vow when I die!

I caress her cheek, then close her eyes,

but I take one more look, for in this mortal world,

this is the last of time.

May her innocence be at peace, as the wicked that spurned her,

let it burn...let it burn, the way it burned her.

Leave her be, and she will pass beyond the walls at dusk,

convalescent from the day before, from the wake I keep,

by mourning for humanity, and that hope will be rising,

give to me, the One's light upon the misty early morning,

for the night from here on out,

is far too dark to see ahead of me,

she was Light-Bearing, she was Love-Bringing,

and may her love, shine through and guide me,

by the One's light and the Love of my life,

may they guide me, and not be lost among the unknowing.

IX. Shadow Lands

I make my way alone...as I have always done,

a lifetime spent, roaming this island,

this land for eternity, broken down, twisted around,

head battered by too many thoughts, too many twists and turns,

I've lost count, I've lost the names and numbers,

mazes and monsters, bridges crossed then bridges burned,

the path is clear, yet leans too far crooked,

not obvious, for I am left standing unsure,

of which forest to dare, which swamp to trample,

all the mountains to climb, fallen down,

the physical damage unrelenting,

the mental damage taking its toll,

no more is there guidance, in this land,

to the light, this land is unknown,

lost to the shadows, still-born in the stream of records,

for I realize that...I have long dreaded the eventual truth,

that I am now one, lost to this scourge,

lost to the fog of sunless, pale eyes,

for I know he watches, I know he changes my path,

plays his game of chess,

for I am the wandering rook, and the queen awaits,

ready to jump me in the dark, when my back is turned,

to see me fail, to leave me lifeless,

my sanity a burning fuse,

for my cool begins to torch, and frustration becomes the better,

the larger, stronger part of this man,

this man lost in shadow land,

lost in Paradise, a hellish torment,

always wanting to bask in the shade,

where the cool sound of the winds rattle the blades of grass,

and the wings a guardian to protect, to shelter,

always feeling...tired...I'm tired of running,

scrambling to get further, tired of going around in circles,

losing my way, losing control,

losing my mind, talking to myself,

for only the brainless, the lifeless,

build their huts and yurts here,

I need to get...over there,

over where that high temple is,

where the black steeples cry out in the midnight air.

Wait, there it is, what I've been searching for,

this has to be the destiny,

the final trek of this unrelenting quest,

take the scent of danger,

and walk upon the heels of nightmares,

that will lead me closer and closer,

towards my destination on the horizon,

a tower of shadows beckons me,

a beacon of moonlight, piercing the thick clouds,

the brooding sight, sends a chill down my spine,

for...this is it, I feel,

I feel I have almost reached the end of the line,

soon...very soon Sepphia,

I will be there to join you,

in the lands of the divine!

X. Into the Temple

I step out of trance, and ascend the stairs,

for the tower looms above, and the temple inside,

up there is where he is...up there in that black spire,

from there is where he rules his kingdom,

he dips his fingers in poison, and sprinkles the acid rain,

corrupting the paradise into a lifeless span of decay,

where time has wasted, where life has been desecrated,

gripping his hand around the world and squeezing,

tighter and tighter, taking the life away,

swallowing the world, devoured into a stomach of darkness,

there is no light, upon this side of the mind,

where shadows rule and truth always lies,

a mirror of false reflection, a dedication to suffering,

torment everlasting, sanity subtracting,

corrupting the shell, a puppet in the show,

a puppet to be cut from the strings and burn in the flames,

once their use is up, once they have served their purpose,

for the temple is merely the surface,

it's the truth, the hideousness that hides underneath,

I vow to scourge this temple, and find what's underneath,

pull the Goat King from his steeple within,

drag him into the flames, and burn him,

be done with him for all time,

tear out his beating heart, and watch as his towers,

his temple and the steeples crumble around him,

the stairs are many, the temple's breath within,

a foul stench of rotting death, a fume of corrosion to the lungs,

but I will enter, I will face this battle head on.

This darkness is forbidding, the pillars and monoliths within,

show signs of ritual and spiritual sacrifice,

blood drips from the Monument of Ghot,

the megalithic dogma in the Goat King's image,

for the hearts of sacrifices, the purging,

are held within Ghot's hands, and upon its face,

a wide grim a smile filled with blood,

for this nightmare of Paradise has enjoyed its feast,

but he shall feast no more,

for nearby, an ancient bell-hammer sits,

I grasp the handle and raise the sledge up high,

"SWISH!" "CRACK!" "SMASH!"

One pound after the other,

one heavy slam after the other,

and the statue sways, and the ebony megalith cracks,

rumble and roar, the megalith begins to fall,

"SLAM!"

I stand aside and watch as the pieces scatter,

as the statue to the Goat King shatters,

and the downfall has begun,

I will see this quest done, the Goat King shall fall,

just as his idol, just as his flock fell to him,

just as he took the lives of my family,

and the will of Sepphia,

corrupting the spirit of my love,

I will see this through, I will place the Goat King's head,

at the end of my spear, and his blood will drip,

his body will lay here, his body will burn here,

for I will let the light shine through,

I will bring upon this land the flame,

I will watch as the light blinds the Goat King,

I will see him fall, he will crawl,

and beg for death, there will be no mercy,

the One may never forgive,

but at the very least...I will not,

nor will anyone else,

be haunted under the Goat King's shadow,

yet I fear...within the mind,

his darkness will linger on, and never be forgotten.

I have been spotted,

my rage has been heard,

the sweat from the heat of my temper,

the scent has been caught upon the wind,

and I am confronted,

intervened by the one,

the protector, the watcher of the fowl one,

Daemonicus...the guardian of the Goat King!

XI. Daemonicus: Guardian of the Goat King

Emerging from the darkness,

apocalypse upon flaming wings,

hoofed feet , just like his master,

protector of the dark one's black gates.

He's come to destroy me,

he's come by the slavery under his master's will,

like all the others, but this beast is different,

he is the epitome of rage and anger,

chaos born from the womb under furious skies,

held up and baptized by damnation,

to serve the Goat King until the end of time.

But he shall feel my spear,

the blade as I slice his head away,

the armor of the One shall protect me,

this harbinger of death shall be defeated!

"You bring with you...the Light of the One,

but he will not help you damned one!

He has abandoned you, deserted you!

Even if you think you will return,

you never will...you'll never see the sun again!"

The wicked laugh of the beast,

echoes through the halls and chambers,

the tower shakes at his terror,

the bricks tremble in his mercy,

but I will not cower before this monstrosity!

I will not give into death,

I will never die, reassure this wicked beast!

And am I damned...well, maybe,

but that will not stop me,

because now this is personal...

The Goat King better prepare for a war,

a slaughter...because once I cleave through this beast,

he better damn well know that the Chosen of the Light,

is coming.

"If you have nothing to say, mortal one,

then I shall destroy you now,

and coat the wall with a new layer of blood!

Then, I will tear your flesh away!"

Daemonicus lunges forth,

the razors upon his battered claw,

swipes across the shield, knocking me back,

a heavy blow, back to my feet, shake it off,

the battle is not over yet.

He strikes again, this time I move to the side,

a quick step, and I slash my sword forward,

and the clawed hand detaches and flies across the temple,

splatters across the wall, as the vile black liquid,

that pumps in this creatures wicked heart,

drizzles down, smoking from an acidic touch,

Daemonicus reels back with a roar of pain and hurt,

gripping the stump,

that now resides at the end of his arm.

In blind rage he rushes back again,

this is where I will do him in.

I bring the blade back, and with a wide swing,

the head is separated from the spine,

the blood begins to melt my sword,

corroding the metal, eating it away,

my ancestors sword, is of no use anymore,

the acid is getting closer, tossing the blade to the floor,

I watch as the rest of the glimmering metal,

the precious artifact of my forefathers disintegrates.

Daemonicus flops to the ground,

tossing and turning, convulsing,

the acid from his poisoned blood leaks all around,

and a large hole is burned into the stone floor,

Daemonicus is taken under, he falls through,

and the sound of a crack and a splatter,

as he hits the bottom and his scaled body splatters.

Daemonicus, guardian, pawn to the Goat King,

exists no more.

Through the darkness, the tunnels lead me along,

to face my final fate,

the obsidian stairs lead up and upwards,

to the spiraling tower,

where he...the black one awaits,

the king of darkness...and lord of internal decay.

Corruption from his lies shall persist no more!

The forked-tongue devil with the head of a goat,

and the horns of a demon,

shall walk in these lands of the shadows no more!

The sun will once more, shine upon these lands,

even if my soul...my life is damned.

I will be sure to not leave this place empty handed,

for upon my spear,

shall be staked the Goat King's head,

and within my hand,

I will hold his beating heart,

and I will tighten my fist, I will smash it,

and only a pulp will remain,

and the blood will ooze through my fingers,

and down my arm,

a trail of this vile, black blood will leave a stain,

a reminder, of this day,

when I confronted the Goat King,

and for the rest of time,

the scrolls and scriptures will be read,

and the angels and the people,

of this liberated world will sing of my name,

the one who confronted, and slayed the Goat King!

XII. Confronting the Goat King

"Come...chosen one... for we have a score to settle,

you and I, come as foe you do,

but maybe...just maybe,

with my guardian dead, there is a place at my side,

I'm willing to forgive the death of my pet,

the death of my protector, not that I really needed one,

but if you leave the light behind, lay down your weapon,

tainted with the blood of my ram,

maybe I'll give you a chance to live...

Rule at my side, oversee my lands,

or I kill you, and return your soul to that sun in the sky,

where he will toss you away to the hounds of Hell,

the dogs of the unforgiving lands..."

And the images of a hell worse than Paradise,

worse than death, fill my mind,

a place where the forgotten ones walk for eternity,

with no purpose, no destination,

a destiny lost to the passing of time.

But I will not give in...

"I refuse to be your lap dog,

your stained pride and joy,

at the tips of your finger, hanging onto my life,

by an unraveling thread, dragged by a leash like a dog,

I will not be the sheep, the animal in this slaughter,

I will not be the ultimate sacrifice lead to the altar!"

"Very well...as you wish,

but you will remember my generosity,

while you're walking upon burning sands,

the oasis for the damned,

prepare..to face your end!"

And the thick, iron doors marked,

by claw marks and adorned with daemonic beings,

twisted by their pain, statues in these dark bowels,

stationary, frozen in time,

abandoned long ago,

by the light of the great divine...open,

a sublime interlude, of what fate has been recorded,

played out, the fate of many,

rests within these halls, on the shoulders of one man,

one journey, who has reached that one destination,

for liberation, for freedom, for divination,

cleanse the night and bring back the sanctuary,

that was once the light, and the burned will be cooled,

the cold will be warmed...

"This...is what I have sworn to do!

I will see to this conclusion, I will see this journey through!"

The doors open, the chambers of the Goat King,

are just ahead, follow the rancid smell of animals and death,

and you will have reached his throne of darkness,

the contributor to the blood tide that rises.

There...just ahead,

the god of darkness,

"...oscuro eclipse lucifer..."

When the darkness eclipses,

casts its shadow over the eye of light,

and the One will be blind,

that will be the day when the Goat King will rule,

ascend the throne to the god of light,

and cast all lands, all territory into an eternal,

sleepless night.

Head lowered, horns pointed,

wings folded, and his glance is at rest,

he meditates, visiting all the nightmares,

he commands the dreams, twists and bends reality,

the lies, when life is not what it seems,

too good to be true, it always is,

but they believed his smile, trusted his voice,

he beckoned them, with promises and security,

the love of a community,

joined under a single divinity,

a dark pact that bound them for all infinity,

and now...the pact will be broken,

the contract inked in blood, and signed by fire,

will be torn asunder and shredded,

tossed away to scatter in the whisper of the winds.

"Come forward...let me see you through my eyes,

the eyes of the Goat King, that is I,

not as Mendes, not as a substitute or a figment of the mind,

no...this is I in the flesh,

as real as you, mortal who stands before me,

who challenges me to a war of fates,

the fate of darkness...versus the fate of the light.

Who will win mortal, for what is our difference?

What is one without the other, the existence of both,

balances the world, for we are one,

we all sleep with the night casting shadows over our eyes, under the moon, that pale eye in the sky,

and we awaken with the day,

the glow of the light...

the sun burns, while the shade cools,

all flee to the shade when the sun punishes,

all have fled to me, for the One has punished,

each and every one of you,

you don't come here by the blessing of the One,

it is your own actions, your own agenda for revenge,

your love for Sepphia, the slaughter of your family,

which I do apologize for by the way,

I did not mean for the situation to escalate the way it did,

but they did attack me first, then the other people,

and I had to defend myself...I had an agenda to go by,

I heard your plea to be with your one true love,

and I was trying to make you an offer,

I wanted to reunite the two of you...ah, but now it's too late,

you killed her, now her essence walks in the oasis,

for your unforgiving One, will never take her back,

he will never take you back either,

so why fight this battle, why escalate this futile war...?"

His eyes open, the red eye, gleaming of an ancient devil,

peering from dark sockets, and thick brows across his forehead,

furrowed in disgust...he can see the look upon my face,

he knows what my answer will be.

"Lies...it all is! I will not be lied to,

I will not fall for your tricks like I did before,

like all the others before,

my family died to protect what they believed in,

to protect me and my eternal soul,

to not cross the sea, and walk upon your shores!

It's because of your corruption that Sepphia is dead,

when I killed her, I freed her from your grasp!

I may have passed beyond the sight,

the protection of the One,

my path may be dark, but there is still a light inside me, a different kind of light guides my path now,

I did not see it before,

but now I understand...I understand what I must do,

a fate that does not involve the decision of the One,

nor you...your hypnotizing call will not get through!

I realize now, that I am alone,

but I have made it this far, so I shall continue,

and if I die here...if I be damned...

then so be it, I will accept what is to become of me!"

He snorts...the steam hot against the chill in the air,

he stands to his feet, his hoofed legs bent back,

he leans over like an old man,

hunched and ready, his wings are spread,

ready to attack, waiting for the pawn,

to make his first move, the wrong move.

"Go on then...what do you wait for?!

Raise your spear and come at me,

take my head if you can,

rip out my heart, if you can,

go on mortal...I give you the first move!"

He bluffs me, I have to plan my moves carefully,

be ready for any tricks,

any sneak attacks, for this is no ordinary being,

the Goat King has many powers, many abilities,

warping, shape-shifting, but the deadliest power of all,

is the decay, the playing with the mind,

making apparitions appear, where they really are not.

I look at him...the eyes of the hated one,

over his head, the clouds of darkness brew,

the swirl round and a haze of smoke and doom,

I then look to the tip of the spear, the blood of the ram,

has corroded the tip,

mixed with the blood of Daemonicus, and it is finished,

darkness cannot undo what darkness has done,

what darkness is, its light that is needed,

the blood...of an enlightened being,

one who would bleed for his cause,

one who would rather bleed to be free,

and I look down to my flesh,

something..within churns,

there is something,

a source within my blood that yearns,

a light that needs to be freed,

turning my skin bright as day,

filling my body, with the spirits of the day.

"If you will not strike! Then I shall kill you now,
and be down with this!"

And from his dark throne,

the lord of darkness, the shade of the light,

descends from above, and upon dark wings he glides,

past the columns and the towers of these,

stone archways that seem to stretch to the skies.

I look up...I look him the eye, and I say to him...

"No...I cannot kill evil...

striking at its heart does no good,

to puncture, only will allow it time,

to lick its wounds,

bleeding of black sludge and foul bile,

No...

I must burn,

light the fire within me,

release the light,

and then you'll burn away...forever!

Feel the fire...and be no more!"

And I take the family sword,

I place the cool steel against my chest,

I make the slice in a vertical line,

the slice is hot, the burn is torture upon my skin,

but I can feel it, I can feel the power....

Release from within!

And the light...let it take him,

let it burn the Goat King,

as it wraps the dead, blue flesh,

of the devil in the shade,

wraps him within a grasp of flames,

as he grasps his stomach and vomits,

all the souls and ectoplasm,

he has kept swallowed and locked away,

the pain wretches and tightens within him,

as he clasps his eyes, and the bulging,

red orbs, melt like candle wax,

against the hot fire, of the light that stings,

thunder roars...the Goat King cries in pain,

he writhes in agony and disdain,

hatred for my blood, hatred for my crime,

my justice to bring him down,

bring this Goat King down!

He says no words...there is only the echo...of the Goat King's,

dying screams, no final curse to be broken,

no penance to be cleansed,

no more land of shadows that was once forsaken,

now...at long last can I say it?

Can I say what has been accomplished,

what my death has awakened?

My sacrifice...the sacrifice...the battle of one man,

the conflict between darkness and light,

has brought about a change...a balance,

as this darkness begins its journey, its shift to light,

and over the shoulder of the furthest hill,

this land of darkness...this Paradise,

has seen...for the first time...in ages,

its first morning light.

Towers crumble, and all this desolation,

I leave behind, for there is no ship to take me home,

and by the grace of the wind,

in her grasp I am taken,

she wisps me across the sea,

to...home,

whether I will be welcome,

whether I will be forsaken is yet to be decided,

by my fate, I am guided,

this is my destiny,

my final destination is what I seek,

my spirit longs to rest,

my soul wishes to sleep,

to find a final resting place after all this war,

after all this death, has faded away,

now but a shade, a faded sprite of what I once was,

a faded image, a portrait painted with dried up paints,

my flesh has cracked, turned to dust,

to blow away,

and to be left here with these remains,

with a soul that wishes to be safe,

will the One grant me sanctuary,

or will he turn me away,

send me to where all the damned men go,

to that place down below.

"So give unto me,

this fate I seek,

there is nothing left,

there is nothing left for me,

nothing left...of ME..."

"One...what is my judgment,

what callus fate awaits,

what awards, what benediction have I forsaken?

Is there any tribulation I have yet to heed,

is there a chance of forgiveness,

is there another way to see, anything else I can be?

Reincarnate me...may I rise from death,

and quench my thirst for eternal slumber,

or shall I prepare myself, to face the torture?

Please maker...tell me! What fate will you bestow,

upon....ME?"

XIII. Ghost in the Embers

"Behold...this pyre of a dying flame,

lift me upon this pyre, and I'll be redeemed,

ignite me, burn me from this body,

take me from this realm, and I'll be free!

I will live on, though I cannot see, I cannot bleed,

I simply long to take the hand, to kiss the lips,

of the one who cares, the one I love,

the one whose loss...I have long despaired,

to see her face, while the last drop of sand,

runs thin, draws the fine line,

of this existence I have left,

the short time I have to exist,

within this world I'm in,

ashes to ashes, now is reborn the phoenix,

face the judge, plead to the jury I'm innocent,

for I represent myself...alone,

to justify this war I fought...this war I won,

the war for my soul...the war for all!"

XIV. An Exile's Last Words

As by Judgment, the decision of the light,

as it was written to be, this...this quest for honor, for peace,

I should have seen the betrayal, I should have known,

this was all a lie, a lie to myself,

who was I deceiving, I should have seen this,

my thoughts foretold,

as I stand in front of the ancient,

the One, the God of all souls new and old,

just as fate and damnation was written,

this...is what I'm told:

"You betrayed me...you've gone beyond,

dare defy me and traverse to the Paradise of the Lost,

you dare go and stand before the Goat King's throne?!

I care not, for sacrifice...for the balance has been disrupted,

and now I must carry, the torch of Love,

as well as the wear the cloak of Hate, to be the good and bad,

to be one in the same...

And now! What say you puny one?

One who has yet to see a lifetime, has yet to be judged,

by me, the all mighty, the all knowing!

For if you would have heeded my code, my law, my word,

you would not receive the fate, the damnation that is to pass,

so...out with it! Any last words?"

I look to the throne, I look to the King of all the sky,

I glare to the Lord of all, and I feel the mouth salivating,

and spit at the One's feet, to curse his name for all eternity.

"You know no love! You know no compassion!

No forgiveness, neither give second chances!

Punish me, I accept my fate, I'll take my damnation gladly,

for I'd rather rule in filth, to struggle along on my own,

to search and find those who have accepted me,

who love me in death as they did in life,

for they have no prejudice that blind them,

they know the rules of fate, and how life works,

that we all make mistakes, and we learn,

we mortals learn from what we've done wrong,

from what we once felt was right,

only to realize the error of our ways,

we act and we reprise, we come back,

we don't hold the grudges nor cast despise and spite!

So I accept my fate, and I'll walk the oasis,

till the end of time, till I find that road,

and I'll cross the line, I'll defeat my obstacles each,

and every time, I'll continue onwards,

for I have all eternity with no chance at a life,

but if that life, is to be filled with fear...of true fear,

even after the sacrifice of casting light upon lies,

and if I am the only liar left,

for I don't deny I have lied to myself time after time,

but what is truth, when a God, a protector,

who wears the robes of light, and preaches love,

casts those who tried...he simply casts them aside,

even after they came to grips that they made a mistake,

and learned the error of their ways!

What...I ask...what kind of a presence are you?

You're no God,

because I can see through your light,

and there is a Goat King, a deceiver inside!"

And I never saw the light again,

for the pits of another fate, another time,

opened up...and I am cast to the wastelands below,

a place without direction,

a place where the damned go.

But somewhere, in all this space and time,

I have killed the light, for no longer will the truth shine,

for the lies always blind, deceive, cheat,

and to defy, to go against the Light we are forced to see,

to blind us with a coating of fantasy and underneath,

that is where the harsh reality stirs.

For this...these places of tunnels and rivers,

of lakes and streams, trees and forests,

desert and sands,

this is what we paint, the picture we create,

to cut the strand of fate,

and from the broken twine, create an existence,

an existence that's yours,

an existence separate from mine.

For we create life, not gods,

we're the liars and the cheats, not demons,

we're the ones who create the world,

create our fate, create the threads of what was,

and what is and will come to pass,

for these are the thoughts, this is the fate,

of a solitary man, who ponders his existence,

as he walks among the ever-changing wasteland,

for like life, this place is ever-changing,

never old or new, just is and is never the same,

constantly shifting between the environment, a realm,

of hot winds and ice-cold rain.

Will I fall to ruin? Will I reign?

Will I become god-like, be the very thing I hate?

Will I walk and ponder the days,

and linger in the past,

question what I should have done,

what I never should have dared?

If this is unbalanced?

And if truth and lies coincide as one,

where is the harmony,

I think, as I walk along,

to search for the beauty of it all,

there has to be something out there,

through the heat and rain, the clouds over my head,

there has to be some form of salvation for me!

XV. WALK THE OASIS

Way down below,

where the harsh winds blow,

I walk this oasis, of thunder, rain, ash, and snow,

heat and lava corrodes the arteries,

as the stain-glassed swords of twisted faith cut me.

There's a place I keep, a place I know,

were only imagination is real,

and the lies in life will never follow,

for in this place, I keep from the winds of Beneath,

I see those faces, familiar and dear to me,

for they are here as well, deep in these oceans,

this oasis where the trodden-over of judgment weep,

and cold winds, the blast of fire...never let them sleep.

Way down below,

and onward, along this trail I go,

where this road will take me, but to nowhere and infinity,

I walk with these familiar faces that I know,

but times change, and no longer do we know,

the times we shared, the times we've known,

for all love and memories are lost in the oasis below.

Deep inside, there's this feeling I know,

that all is lost and there is nowhere left to go,

upon mountains of blood-red, I gaze into the darkness below,

I cannot see what's to come, I can no longer see,

those faces behind me, those faces I once held dear in memory,

for the shadows envelop,

the skies abound, and the earth below,

I guess I'm heading forward, for there is nowhere else to go.

I begin to think, to ponder on the lives of old,

a past life where a future of glory had been foretold,

but now it's clear to me, now I see,

my fate forever onward, is this frozen state of lingering,

the more I move, the more I hurt,

the more I stand still, the frozen ice of the oasis burns,

the less I sleep, the less I do,

has this...is this it...is this,

the child's fairytale that has been assumed,

to bask in the darkness, deep below,

to be banished from the light, to bask in the shadows,

to age forever, to never know, to remember the youth,

my existence ends, less than a lifetime too soon.

And so the winds blast my skin,

and I age yet another day, a self-conflict I'll never win,

the lives above pass me by,

the memory, the passion of my deeds, my heroism,

buried here with me, down here beneath the murky tides,

knee-deep upon a sinking road,

the further I go, the less there is,

there's nothing left of me to show,

and I look back, for none have followed,

I walk alone a solitary man.

And two legs turn to three, the eternal clock rotates,

and as the sands run down, I crawl upon all four,

no food, no water, no shelter, no grass,

my time is up it seems, for all that's left is to rest,

dragged myself for miles, nothing to show,

scars, scratches, bruises, and blisters,

skin so numb, so cold...but the sun, that sun hurts,

mocks me, like life, as I traverse along the edge,

of a road, of lifetimes, I no longer know,

all I want to do is sleep now,

for this young man is now weary and old,

there is no love, no family, no one to hold,

I just want to be one with life again,

I wish I could bask in what's left of this dying soul.

But that's existence...when shadows die,

the light has the chance to scorch sand and sky,

burn flesh and blind eyes, there are no tears to cry,

for the heart, like my skin,

has shriveled up and died,

there are no feelings left, for when shadows fell,

and the daylight, the rays of hope betrayed,

something...something within this man,

something died in me that day...that day....

XVI. Existence

Burn away, the flesh on me,

I'm no longer this man,

shelter from the pain is all I seek.

Walked for miles, seems eons have passed,

when was the last time,

I tasted food, walked upon the grass.

And I'm aware of this curse, my life,

maybe things will be better,

in death...

I killed all that I loved, to free my land,

only to walk alone,

here I stand as a solitary man.

My throat is dry, my only water,

is when I cry, this shelter I seek,

is nowhere, this has all been a lie.

And I know I can never go back,

I can never change what is done,

however, there is another option, an escape...

I don't know, where this damned man will go,

Paradise is dead, the One light has lied,

no protection, no divinity, no hope, no inheritance,

nowhere else to go!

Can I take another step?

This existence is not for me.

Can I find peace after death?

Because this existence was never for me.

A quest for worth, turned into guilt,

to save the lives of all,

only to see the kingdom fall.

With the Goat King slain, has anything changed?

All is still lost,

all that was, has all faded away.

And I know I can never go back,

I can never change what is done,

but is there a faint chance,

that out of all of this...something has been won?

A soul never to rest in peace,

I wish this existence was never to be,

but fate is a warning our hearts keep,

this existence was meant to be...

"All that's left, after the conflict ceases,

is nothing but scars and bruises..."

www.ingramcontent.com/pod-product-compliance
Lightning Source LLC
LaVergne TN
LVHW041211080426
835508LV00011B/915